MW00527473

The Systems Thinker

Essential Thinking Skills For Solving Problems, Managing Chaos,

and Creating Lasting Solutions in a Complex World

Written by Albert Rutherford

professional person should be sought. The author shall not be liable for damages arising therefrom.

The fact that an individual, organization of website is referred to in this work as a citation and/or potential source of further information does not mean that the author endorses the information the individual, organization to website may provide or recommendations they/it may make. Further, readers should be aware that Internet websites listed in this work might have changed or disappeared between when this work was written and when it is read.

First Printing, 2018.

Printed in the United States of America

Email: albertrutherfordbooks@gmail.com

Table of Contents

Introduction

"It isn't what we know that gives us trouble, it's what we know that ain't so." – Will Rogers

As humans, we are incredibly intelligent beings. This can be both a blessing and a sort of curse as there are many times when we revert to our "teenage ways" and think we know everything we need to about life when nothing could be further from the truth. If there is anything my time on Earth and my teaching career has taught me, it's how little I really know. As someone who, until recently, was responsible for educating adults and helping them get their start in the world, I am acutely aware it was impossible for me to teach my students everything they will need to know in their lives. The best I could hope for was to give them a thirst for and love of learning that would inspire them to be lifelong learners: always open-minded enough to receive and analyze new information even when it differs from their beliefs and the tools they need to find and recognize good reputable sources.

Unfortunately, there are many people who think they have everything figured out and know all the answers. This belief can be to their great detriment. Take the Nazca civilization for example.[1] They had by and large been thriving in

---

[1] The Nazca culture was an archaeological culture that thrived from c. 100 BC to 800 CE in the southern coast of Peru between the river valleys of Ica and the Rio Grande de Nazca drainage. The Nazca left behind a rich variety of crafts and technologies such as ceramics, textiles, and geoglyphs—today known as the Nazca Lines. They also built an imposing underground aqueduct system that still works today. Extracted from *The Nasca by Helaine Silverman and Donald A. Proulx. Blackwell Publishers. Malden. 2002.*

the desert ecosystem of southern Peru between around 100 BC and 800 CE when they disappeared about 1500 years ago. While their disappearance has been somewhat of a mystery, scientists now theorize that the choices they made as a civilization ultimately could have been avoided and lead to the destruction of their entire civilization.

The Nazca civilization lived in the desert where there's a delicate balance between living things that ensure survival. Despite having built a strong and successful civilization, they made a fateful decision that lead to their decline. Their environment was home to the *Prosopis pallida* or huarango tree which was special in that it helped to make the soil more fertile and better able to hold in moisture as well as support the irrigation system the Nazca had built. The huarango tree had the deepest roots of any tree in their area, which helped to hold the soil in place and keep it from being eroded by rivers and wind. In addition, as with all living things, it was part of nature's delicate balance.

The Nazca civilization made the aforementioned fateful decision to become an agricultural society. While that alone seemed like a sound decision, it led to a chain of unfortunate events for the once great and powerful civilization. They made the transition to agriculture rather quickly, cutting down many of the huarango trees to make way for planting crops like cotton and maize. They cut down so many of the trees that they lost the benefits these trees had to offer. When storms like *El Niño* brought floods, their roots were not there to help hold the soil in place. The irrigation did not continue to work as well as it had and the trees weren't there to keep needed moisture in the soil to help their crops grow and the soil was no longer fertile. The Nazcas were no longer successful in growing their crops, thus food became scarce, there was not enough to feed everybody so their civilization slowly disappeared as their people died.[i]

One can't help but wonder if they had understood the science of the huarango trees and considered the long-term consequences of their choices, they might have made different decisions that would not have led to such a devastating outcome for the Nazca civilization.[ii]

The story of the Nazca civilization, while is tragic, is not unique. The history of planet Earth is rich with stories of extinction and so it is, too, with changes that led to those extinctions made by us, the *homo sapiens*. As I said at the beginning of this book, we are incredibly intelligent beings. This sometimes is a blessing; other times is a curse. Usually it is a curse for other species and for the generations who come after the perpetrators of environmental change. One man is not likely to see the long-term consequences of his actions in his lifetime.

How could the simple farmer of Mesopotamia or Mesoamerica know his system of accounting and keeping track of his crops would result in e-books? How could the ancient scientist know that his experiment with metal alloys would result in the atomic bomb? To see the long-term impacts of these changes, thousands of years had to pass and additional developments had to be made.

The changes of the modern age are happening much more quickly. Thanks to science and engineering, changes reveal themselves faster. Biochemical and biological engineering helps to increase the quantity of food available. Norman Borlaug, for example, was an agricultural researcher, and developed a high yield type of wheat that was so successful in Mexico, India, and Pakistan that it earned him the Nobel Peace Prize for preventing more than a billion people from starvation deaths.[iii] Genetic engineering helps us produce food at higher yields and promises better life for our children, and physicists can create nuclear power to supply energy to our homes.

Let's take a closer look at the timeline of these innovations. The first biological engineering program started in 1966 at the University of California, San Diego. Genetic engineering, as we know it, being a direct manipulation of DNA by humans, has only existed since the 1970s. The first nuclear power plant opened its gates in 1954, in Obninsk, USSR. We can clearly feel the benefits of these innovations today, even though they happened in our lifetime (the lifetime of fossils like myself nevertheless). What's more, we've already started feeling the *secondary impact* of some of these innovations.

Pesticides created by biochemical engineering have killed pests short term, only allowing many of them to develop pesticide resistance. At the same time, however, the number of other, untargeted insects dropped significantly like of wild bees.[iv] Norman Borlaug, who has been considered the father of modern agriculture, got a lot of criticism from environmentalists and nutritionists for the Green Revolution as it produced a lot of negative side effects such as increased rates of cancer in rural areas, water and soil depletion, and dependence on fossil fuels etc.[v]

Due to the heat nuclear reactors release, the spawning pattern of fish in those areas has changed.

Not only science and engineering-related changes have accelerated to show their primary and secondary impact. Social, political, and economic changes operate on a higher speed too. For our ancestors, it took hundreds of years to switch from a hunter-gatherer lifestyle to an agricultural based society. How many years did it take to create a society where we can't imagine living without high speed internet? Ten? I don't even want to talk about "internet" as a stand-alone term anymore. Could you imagine going back to dial up?

How have these changes affect us so fast? How did they affect the environment? And more importantly, what are the changes and consequences that are most likely to happen in the next twenty, fifty, or one hundred years? Future generations are all going to have kyphosis because we spend all our time hunched over the phone. I don't even dare thinking about a more distant future.

Had I been imaging about the next hundred years in 1918, I would have never have guessed what 2018 would've looked like.

Systems thinking is a paradigm shift in the way we view the world. A system is a group of things that are interconnected and demonstrate their own behavior pattern over time. Traditionally, we have been taught to look at things in a linear analytical fashion in order to search for clear cause and effect relationships. If the car runs out of gas, the car stops. Easy, right? But how could we explain with the same logic the multidisciplinary changes nuclear power plants create? How could we say matter-of-factly that if the nuclear reactor releases heat, the spawning habits of fish will change? Can we explain this phenomenon purely through biology? Or chemistry? Or physics? No, we can't give a proper explanation with a reductionist, mono-disciplinary approach.

Systems thinking takes a different approach. When we think in systems, we slow down and dig deeper, trying to find solutions and explanations to given phenomena. Systems thinking encourages us to look at events and patterns that occur in our lives and around us by focusing on the connection and relationship between the system's parts instead of only looking at the individual parts in isolation. It encourages observing the interconnections of the parts.

Systems thinking leads us away from trying to come up with a quick fix to a problem in favor of considering the long-term consequences our actions may cause. It supports a deeper level of understanding than we typically take the time to seek.

In our fast-paced and complex society today, the information we think we know with certainty can quickly become obsolete. We have to be open and receptive to all of the new knowledge that can be afforded to us through science and technology and be willing to view it through our systems thinking lens. This is so we can rid ourselves of the information that simply isn't true, and be ready to face the future confident we are armed with the best information currently available. This way allows us to make a more accurate prognosis for the future. This being said, we have to consider as many factors in each case. Many of the big issues I was tackling in my introduction aren't black and white, wrong or right issues. They have a lot of gray area and multiple point of views to consider. For example, many people considered Norman Borlaug a hero, also many people considered his "Green Revolution" technique to be responsible for deforestation and devastating to the soil in those areas his technique was practice. Many people don't agree with bioengineering foods at all and argue that the region that were saved a billion starvation death could also not economically support those lives, so Borlaug circumvented a kind of cruel natural selection. My point is that cases like Borlaug's aren't as simple as was he a hero for saving lives and creating a kind of wheat that could be cheaply and easily grown or was he a monster responsible for terrible environmental crimes.

Taking more viewpoints into consideration, and examining them through systems thinking lens can help to prevent or rectify some tragedies, we can try to fix the greatest social problems with a higher chance of success, and ultimately, we can find deeper understanding and empathy in our experiences with other cultures.

Let's begin by taking a closer look at the evolution of systems thinking…

Chapter 1: Where Is Systems Thinking Coming From?

Science, as we think of it today, has come a long way from where it used to be. In the past, science, by and large, tended to look at events as individual occurrences that seemingly happened in isolation. The different fields of science would concentrate on the event without trying to see how it fit into the bigger picture. It would be akin to carefully studying, examining, and reporting on what you had learned and observed from an individual puzzle piece without bothering to relate any information or even study how it fit into the whole puzzle.

Through the years, the different fields of science have evolved, and there has been a paradigm shift in the way we look at things scientifically. We are still concerned with carefully examining individual events, but the shift has now been toward making the whole picture a priority as well, instead of only concentrating one part of that event. We understand that things are often more interdependent than independent from one another.

I would also add that the world in general drifted toward a scientific working togetherness and the inclusion of different specialties. The different fields of science we mix bring in other areas to cover every possible aspect of the field of research. For example, if you have a specific environment you're studying you'd have someone for the vegetation, someone for the soil samples, someone for any water samples, specialists for animals - both marine and land...

You can see the same phenomenon in academia today. When a faculty member is going to take on a research grant or project he or she is never alone. The research includes at the very least staff and students to gather data and manage the project. Often the faculty is working on the grant with other faculties so we might end up having a special education faculty. For example we can have a bilingual education faculty on a grant to study the needs of the bilingual refugees who may require special education services or to make sure if they are getting proper services.

Let's take a few fields of science and look at the changes they've gone through over time.

Physics

Traditional, classic physics focused on breaking things down into their smallest pieces to examine and study them, and believed that these small pieces would act in the same way whether they were operating in isolation or as part of a larger and more complex group. Things were viewed through the lens of being a haphazard collection of atoms that behaved in a way determined by the laws of nature. This kind of worldview was reinforced when statistical laws rooting in Boltzmann's derivation of the second principle of thermodynamics took the place of the previously presented deterministic laws.

Modern physics has shifted to focus more on problems of organization and how things may be interrelated. Scientists working in this field are trying to solve these types of problems in the areas of structural chemistry and atomic physics among others.

Biology

Much in the same vein of physics, biology has been evolving in a very similar way. In the past, biology was largely aiming to break down living things to their smallest parts: cells so they could be studied. The thought was that parts of organisms could be viewed in isolation for the purposes of understanding how they worked. An organism is considered to be the multitude of cells working together. Organismic conceptions have gained bigger importance as modern biology has evolved. It became crucial and necessary to study not only individual parts, but also the relation of organizations coming from interaction dynamics and behavior difference. Like physics, a more modern view of biology sees the value in studying how the parts of living things are interconnected and fit together in the bigger picture of the organism as a whole.

Medicine

Similarly, medicine was once most concerned with examining illness at the cellular level. While there is certainly value in this, modern medicine has also evolved to see the importance of viewing the patient as a whole instead of simply a collection of individual parts. There are doctors who offer house calls. Patients can seek out a doctor who listens to them. The US medical schools teaches bedside manners to young doctors so they can relate to their patient as a person not just a body on a table.

Sociology

Like all of the other scientific disciplines previously discussed, sociology too, has undergone an evolution where it has moved away from merely thinking of society as a sum total of individuals that were added together. In the past, classical economy defined society as the sum of its individuals. Modern sociology rather looks at a society, a country, a nation as a whole which gives the basis of the concept of collectivism. This shift often creates unpleasant consequences for the individual as the individual needs get "sacrificed" for the good of the community and country. Nevertheless, in today's analysis, the emphasis is on the interaction of units above the individual like countries, economic clusters, etc.[vi]

What do all of these scientific disciplines have in common? They have moved away from a nearly complete focus on studying only the smallest parts of things to expanding their focus to include how those parts are connected to and dependent upon one another. This is true whether they are studying physical things, living things, or groups of people. What has caused this change of perspective throughout the scientific spectrum?

Is there an isomorphic law,[2] or guiding principle that extends beyond one field of science to span and connect multiple different fields of science?

---

[2] A direct translation of isomorphic means literally "same form."

As we have seen in the examples above, many scientific fields shifted from deconstructing elements to its particles to analyzing the dynamics and working togetherness of multiple elements. This shift seems to be present regardless of the scientific field. The question becomes, what is the driving force guiding these change? Is there a comprehensive stimulus that triggered this shift in many scientific fields? Is there an isomorphic law at work that made this shift possible?

The focus on examining whether there are identical laws that run through all the different scientific fields is a relatively new approach. Until recently, it would have been virtually unheard of to look for similarities between atoms, molecules, people, bacteria, animals, and physical objects across all scientific disciplines. We are coming to find out that there are more similarities among them than we could have ever expected.

Where do these isomorphic similarities come from? Ludwig von Bertalanffy, the father of general systems theory, identified three reasons for the different fields of study to share the same isomorphic natural laws:

- There is a finite number of scientific laws or equations for solving things, so it makes sense that we use and adapt what is available to us all across the scientific disciplines.

- We can apply these laws into our world.

- Natural laws, like the exponential law, can prove to be true across a variety of situations and scientific fields. It is applicable in more than one instance as it holds true in the same type of system, even when the elements that exist within the systems are quite different. In the case of exponential law, or the Law of

Exponents,[3] if the exponent is negative, the same rule applies to the decay of oxygen, the loss of body substance in a starving organism, molecular reactions, population decrease, financial decrease, or skill acquisition based by effort and time devoted. If the exponent is positive, an exponential growth can be observed in all the aforementioned areas. The subjects involved in each scenario are fairly different. The process that leads to the general decay or growth are also different, yet the Law of Exponents produces the same outcome. The Law of Exponents stays true in the case of

---

[3] "The principle that growth or decay of some physical quantity is at a rate such that its value at a certain time or place is the initial value times e raised to a power equal to a constant times some convenient coordinate, such as the elapsed time or the distance traveled by a wave; there is growth if the constant is positive, decay if it is negative." *From McGraw-Hill Dictionary of Scientific & Technical Terms, 6E. S.v. "exponential law." Retrieved August 9 2018 from* *https://encyclopedia2.thefreedictionary.com/exponential+law*

chemistry, biology, economics, demography, or individual skill acquisition efforts. [vii]

The transition of thinking from part to whole across the disciplines has made General System Theory possible. When Ludwig von Bertalanffy was first establishing the General System Theory, he was hesitant to call it a theory because he didn't want to have it face the typical constraints that scientific theories of his time usually faced. He didn't want it to be confined to one field of science or one area of study. He saw it more as a way to look at whole systems and wanted it to be free to be used across multiple disciplines. He wanted it to be a more modern way of looking at the world and a new unifying, direction for science to take.

Bertalanffy's theory was a new approach that came about during his studies following World War II and focused on the similarities across all areas of science and didn't place any more importance on one field of science than the others.

He recognized that the phenomena we observe in the world have much in common when considered as a whole rather than just parts in isolation, and he took a major step toward the way we use systems thinking today.

The General System Theory had three main goals:

- To bring together the analytical way of investigating things as well as provide a scientific method for looking at the organismic domain by focusing on similarities between different scientific disciplines.

- To find connections between systems that, on their face, appear to be very different but upon deeper reflection have a lot in common.

- To show facts and values in science can and should peacefully and harmoniously coexist hand-in-hand in scientific investigations by adhering to a humane code of ethics.[viii]

The General System Theory sought to make generalizations about whole systems. It did not want to abandon the foundation of knowledge of each individual field of science. It aimed to be transdisciplinary with each field bringing its expertise to the table; to be actively engaged in working together to create a common base of methods and knowledge for all of the scientific disciplines to share while still being true to each individual discipline's facts as well.

It was an effort to "expand the tent" if you will to be more inclusive of knowledge from all areas. It was an effort to not be so focused on the little pieces that we couldn't also see the bigger picture. Bertalanffy didn't want us to miss the forest for the trees.

Today systems thinking – while its methodology has changed and refined through the years - is actively used in politics, economics, sociology, demographic analysis, and environmental studies among others.

Chapter 2: Today's Problems

We tend to view objects through an analytical, logical lens when we are carefully studying them in small, understandable pieces as we are looking for cause and effect relationships or are trying to solve problems. It is through this lens that we sometimes run the risk of seeing problems as being inflicted upon us rather than accepting responsibility for our part in creating them. This is our nearsighted view of our world, where our clear focus is only on the little parts that are closest to us, and the big picture remains fuzzy. In contrast, there are times when our view is more farsighted, and we focus more clearly on the bigger picture.

Before we even knew how to think logically, we were able to subconsciously operate complex systems. We are a complex system, after all. We have intuitively built up this system-our body-with all its complexity, without any analysis or logic. Our body is a naturally self-maintaining system. It needs hydration and food, of course, but we don't need to think about how to digest, divide and absorb the nutrients and so on. Every living thing, from plants to animals, is a complex system. It seems we were born knowing instinctively how to relate to and understand complex systems at least to a basic degree.

Although as a discipline, systems thinking is fairly new, let me prove to you its basic principles have been around for a long time. Some wisdom grew out of the heads of our ancestors long before systems thinking was a "thing." Let's look at a few examples:

Have you ever heard the proverb "A stitch in time saves nine?" This wise saying tells us that it is better to take a little time right away to deal with a problem because if you put it off until later, you might find that the problem has grown to be much larger and more difficult to solve. This would certainly be supported by systems thinkers who know that there are feedback delays present in complex systems which can prevent us from knowing about a problem in a timely manner. This often means that by the time we become aware of a problem, it is already quite challenging to address.

"To the victor belongs the spoils" may be another saying with which you are familiar. It points out that when someone wins, they receive a reward that goes with it. Often this reward makes winning again in the future more likely. Systems thinkers agree that reinforcing feedback loops reward those who are victorious in competitions, and it is those very rewards which increase the likelihood that the same people will continue to win, which will effectively serve to eliminate most competitors.[ix]

Warren Buffet wisely said "Never test the depth of the river with both of your feet." This wisdom reminds us of the importance of protecting ourselves from unfortunate events by trying to be stable and diversified. If we put all of our efforts, hopes, and resources into one area and something bad happens, we will quickly find ourselves on shaky ground. Systems thinkers understand this as well. They know that diversity is a key component of shielding ourselves from vulnerability and a lack of stability should things go wrong.

Today's world view and its problems

Once we started to move from a largely agricultural society to a more industrial one, we began to rely more on scientific thinking and logic rather than our instincts and holistic approaches to reasoning. There are times when this served us well in our history. We were able to meet our transportation and shipping needs, find the cure for some diseases, and rally together behind many common causes worthy of fighting for. The solutions to our immediate problems, however, resulted in new problems that are embedded deeply in the complex system. Overpopulation, hunger, poverty, and economic swings persist in spite of analytical thinking.

Intuitive thinking encourages us to place blame for problems outside of ourselves instead of being open minded enough to examine how we may have contributed to the problem and how we need to be part of the solution. We've become so focused on finding a quick that we don't engage in the systems thinking that would help us evaluate the consequences that have resulted from our choices and actions. When we don't fully think things through from multiple angles, we often cause unintended negative consequences. Solely thinking in a logical manner doesn't account for those truly complex system problems that elude our efforts to find solutions. Problems like our opioid addiction epidemic, finding the cure for diseases like cancer and Alzheimer's, poverty, and rising suicide rates have not been solved despite all of the current effort of multiple groups looking to tackle these incredibly complex and challenging efforts such as interventionists and drug recovery leaders, scientists on the cutting edge of medical research, job training groups that teach skills to help bring families out of generational poverty, and training groups such as Q.P.R aimed at training everyday people to recognize the symptoms of someone contemplating suicide. That's because these problems are systems problems present in multiple fields at once. Just because you try to fix the problem in one field, it will still persist in other fields.

For example, a country making drugs illegal or harder to obtain may have fixed the drug problem on a political level, but it can often cause more damage in other fields. Let's take drug addiction and drug-related violence as an example. Banning drugs forces dealers to sell drugs illegally, boosting organized crime rates and the price of the drugs. The users now have to pay higher prices of the products that often means they will spend their last buck on drugs. While we can say that politically the drug question was handled, the problem itself didn't disappear following the passage of new laws and policies. Are politicians and lawmakers to blame in this situation? Or drug dealers? Or the users? Who is responsible for this problem? And more importantly who will solve this problem?

If I had the answer to these questions, I'd probably be a millionaire and hold speeches at UN conferences. The solution to drug addiction and drug-related violence won't be fixed by finding a scapegoat and casting blame on it. Policies that follow a cause-and-effect logic won't solve it either. The solution will come to light as the result of intuitive, empathetic listening and problem solving. When we find the wisdom and guts to restructure the system itself, we will be able to undo something that system structure deficits produced.

If we only do what we have always done, we will only continue to get the same results we have always gotten in the past. As Albert Einstein said, the definition of insanity is doing the same thing and expecting a different result.

Our world changes so quickly, and we are more interconnected and interdependent than we have ever been before. We have to stop looking to place blame and wait for an outside source to improve our situation. We need to engage in systems thinking so we can get to the root of the problem, looking at both the parts and the system as a whole, so we can craft real solutions. It is only then that we will truly create the change we wish to see in the world.

The blind men and the elephant

You may have heard of the ancient Indian story about the blind men and the elephant. The story is about a group of blind men who have encountered an elephant for the first time. They try to understand what is in front of them and create a picture in their minds. Each man touches one part of the elephant such as the ear, leg, trunk or tusk. No two men touch the same part. When the blind men try to describe what they have felt to each other, their descriptions are vastly different. Each man could not imagine why the descriptions the others gave were so dissimilar to his own personal experience and assumed that the other men must either be wrong or lying.

This story teaches us an important lesson about systems thinking: it is impossible to understand a system and the way it behaves if our focus is only on the individual elements within it. If we hope to really learn about a system, we need to see the system as a whole and study the way the different elements interact and are interdependent with each other.

Chapter 3: Quick Systems Overview

Let's start at the beginning. What is a system? A system is a group of interconnected elements that work together to achieve a common purpose or function. In order to consider something a system, we need to have three things:

1. Elements;
2. Interconnections;
3. Purpose or function.

If even one of those items is missing, we don't have a system.

Let's look at a system we all depend on every day. Our skeletal system is made up of the elements of bones, joints, ligaments, tendons, and cartilage that are all interconnected. The skeletal system has a vital purpose that includes providing a framework and support for the body, working with our muscular system to help our bodies move, making blood cells for the body, and protecting our organs and soft tissues among other functions without which we wouldn't be able to survive.

By our definition, it may seem like absolutely everything is a system, but this isn't the case. I recently stopped at a gas station located across the street from a gravel pit. As I filled up my car, I watched as large trucks came in, carrying rocks or hauling them away. The number of rocks varied with each load that entered or left, but as far as the rock quarry, the rocks weren't interconnected with one another and they weren't working toward achieving a common purpose. They were just rocks piled up at a gravel pit. They were not a system.

Systems can change and react to the environment around them. They respond to changes and find ways to survive when things go wrong. This is true whether it is a living or nonliving system.

The parts of a system:

The elements

These are the individual parts of the system and are usually the easiest to identify. The elements can often be seen and touched, but sometimes they are intangible as well. The elements of a family are the individual family members, but there are also intangible feelings and bonds involved like love, loyalty, a sense of belonging, and pride among other things. The elements of a rose, for example, are the petals, stem, roots, leaves, and thorns.

The interconnections

The elements work together and depend on one another through interconnections. In our example of the rose system, the stem provides the flower with support and helps to transfer nutrients and water throughout the plant. The roots provide the flower with water, the petals attract the pollinators to the flower to allow for reproduction, and the thorns provide protection from predators. All of these interconnections work together to help the rose survive. If any of the elements do not do their part, the flower will not thrive.

Sometimes interconnections are not as easy to immediately spot because they are not visible, but are instead a flow of information. Information flow in a system results in decisions being made and actions being taken. When we are looking closely at a system we can see these information flows occurring. For example, when a teacher evaluates a student, there is an information flow happening between the two elements of the evaluation system: the teacher and the student. The teacher listens closely, and based on how well the student knows the material, he decides the fitting grade.

To observe hidden interconnections, you can think back to the traditional family system. Children in a family may make decisions based on sibling rivalry or how they think a parent will react. For example, based on the specific relationship they have with each parent and the parent's personality, a child is likely to go to one parent over another when they want to ask for money or to share the news that they received a bad grade on their report card. They are likely to go to a certain parent to ask for help with homework based on how well the parent can explain things to them or which parent is stronger in math, science, or whatever subject the project is in. Children may decide where they would like to go to college based on where their siblings went or whether they want to be closer to or more independent from their parents or even based on their parents' alma mater.

A government can't make good policy changes without information and research on a problematic subject. Just because they know there is a problem doesn't mean they can take unfounded action without having the necessary data, research, and the voices of the relevant constituents being heard. Without enough information, making a decision is just as safe as relying on blindfolded, dart throwing monkeys to hit the center of the dartboard. And since bad political decisions are likely to cost a politician his or her seat in office, he or she is likely to have all the research possible and all the data needed before casting any political votes or changing any policies.

In a system, just knowing about a problem's existence isn't enough to lead to an informed decision. You also need to know things like what positive outcomes the change may create throughout the entire system, what types of consequences may accompany the decision, and what help or materials are available. This is why understanding the interconnections of a system is so vital; the deeper the understanding of the subject, the better the chances of reaching the desired outcome.

Function or purpose

When it comes to systems, the word function is usually used to describe nonhuman systems while purpose is used when discussing human systems. The denomination can be mixed, though, since many systems are made of both human and nonhuman elements.

The function or purpose of a system isn't always clearly spelled out in the same way that a mission statement or goals or objectives might be for a company. Often the best way to really know what the purpose of a system is, is to observe the system in action and watch its behavior over time. You know, "actions speak louder than words." This is very true when it comes to determining the purpose of a system. An example of actions versus words within a system would be a politician who makes many campaign promises about his or her purpose for while running for office, but it will be their behavior displayed once in office that reveals their true purpose.

The function of almost every system is the will and work to ensure its own survival. Think back to our example of the system of the rose. The petals have the job of attracting pollinators to the plant so that it can reproduce and ensure that there will be more roses in the future. At the same time, the thorns on a rose serve to protect it so that the rose system wards off predators. In our example of the politician, he or she must make campaign promises to attract financial contributors and voters to ensure success in a primary or the continuation to hold office once they are elected.

It can also happen that the real purpose of the system ends up being something that was not wanted or willfully perpetuated by any of the elements. When this happens, it may result in an unintended consequence that no one really wanted. It is also possible for systems to have more than one purpose at the same time and for the elements within the system to be working toward different purposes. Let's look at the example of high stakes standardized testing in public schools to demonstrate how this can happen. I will list some of the elements at play and their *intended* individual purposes:

- Politicians want to demonstrate to their constituents that they are invested in the education of public school children.

- Parents want their children to be academically successful and achieve high test scores.

- School districts want to receive higher scores so they can be competitive with other nearby districts and attract more students, better teachers, – and more federal and state funds.

- Teachers want their students to do well as a means of job security, and in some cases, to earn merit pay.

- Students want to do well and avoid being retained in a grade or having to take remedial or summer school classes because they want to avoid parental disappointment and social ridicule among other reasons.

- Companies who sell educational materials want to make money by writing the high-stakes tests, providing practice or remedial materials, creating software programs and technology, writing textbooks, and providing staff development programs for teachers. They develop measures for students that test for autism, learning disabilities, emotional disturbance, etc.

What started as a genuine effort to ensure that students were being taught the curriculum assigned to them and received extra help if they weren't meeting certain benchmarks, quickly turned into a dysfunctional system of pressure, money poorly spent, and chronic teacher burnout because the original purpose was weighed down and obliterated by all of the sub-purposes competing with one another within the larger system. The elements became so concerned about their own individual purposes that the unifying purpose got lost.

Today, high stakes, standardized testing is quite controversial. We still have the same problems in the education system that we did before standardized testing began because the tests have been unable to solve them. But now we have new problems as well that came along as unintended negative consequences.

Students are experiencing significant anxiety over testing not to mention that the measures of the tests are also fairly problematic and they are rarely indicators of potential or ability. Many parents and teachers are alarmed at how much of the school day is spent teaching to the test or taking tests and how much of the district's budget is spent on testing materials. Some parents are opting out of having their children take the tests altogether. Teaching has become more competitive and less cooperative as teachers are now trying to outperform each other to ensure job security and merit pay rather than supporting fellow teachers and helping students who are academically at risk. Many teachers have left the profession and fewer professionals are choosing to enter it right out of college, creating a teacher shortage.[x]

Low performing schools are penalized by having their state funds taken away, when these are arguably the schools the need it the most, or the state education department goes in and takes control of the school. As a result, well-performing teachers often leave the school in frustration seeking better opportunities and thereby they are leaving the schools that have the most minorities, learning disabled, or economically disadvantaged students who'd need well-trained educators the most.[xi xii]

The sub-systems and sub-purposes within the larger system began to work against one another and the result was a system that is no longer delivering its original purpose: having well educated, but also socially normative and happy children. The system has instead created negative consequences that no one ever wanted or intended.

To maintain a successful system, the sub-purposes and the main purpose have to be kept in harmony. Later in this book we'll see examples on how can we bring people with different sub-purposes to the table and work toward a compromised agreement.

What changes a system the most?

Usually, changing the elements has the smallest impact on the system. If we stick to the school system example we can easily see that exchanging the teachers, staff, administrators, and students with new ones, would still easily allow us to recognize the system as being a school. The same rules would apply to the school, of who is in it.

Changing the interconnections, on the other hand, has a far greater impact on the system as a whole. Even if we didn't change any element, changing some interconnections can alter the system to the point of being unrecognizable. If a public school was changed to a private school where students were required to pay tuition to attend and only students with specific skill levels or the ability to pay were accepted, the system would be very different. In such a case students might not worry about standardized tests that have problematic measures, and they might have their pick of the best teachers. The teachers might be religiously affiliated and be required to adhere to a very strict code of conduct. One private school fired its teacher because she got pregnant prior to her marriage.[xiii] She worked for a private catholic high school so that was not a behavior the school wanted the teacher to endorse and thus terminated her.

Such kind of private schools might also lack diversity, as lower SES students are more like to be people of color. A school in Louisiana had a policy against hair extensions that was deemed racist and specifically targeting to exclude black girls from the school. This policy has been rescinded just last month, in August, 2018.[xiv]

Changing the purpose or function of a system can produce even more drastic results. If the purpose of a school is no longer to educate students what is the purpose? What if the purpose was to only cater to children while their parents are working without teaching them at all? Or what if only those children who specifically ask for it would be educated?

All components within a system: elements, interconnections, and function or purpose are equally important to the success of the system, and they all have their own jobs to do. Ironically, it is the part of the system that is usually the hardest to recognize, the function or purpose, which has the biggest influence on the system's behavior. The most easily recognizable parts of a system – the elements – often play the smallest role in determining a system's behavior, but this isn't always the case. In a school system example, changing the headmaster might have a large impact on defining the system if changing him or her also resulted in the purpose or interconnections being changed. Just think of how much Hogwarts changed after Dolores Umbridge replaced Albus Dumbledore…

Stocks and Flows

Stocks are the building blocks of any system. They are the elements that can be measured. In our school system example, the stocks would be the number of students, the test scores, the amount of time or money spent on testing, the number of textbooks available for different subjects, the stress and anxiety levels of the students and teachers, and the number of voters who supported a politician's position on education are all examples of stocks. As you can see, stocks can be living beings just as much as inanimate objects or conceptual things.

Diagram 1: Stock and Flow

Stocks change over time based on the flows. In a school system, students can move in or out of a district, the number of students in schools depends on the birth rate demographics, ages of the people living in the community, and the amount of money going into the district is dependent on the tax rates approved by the legislature and voters. The test scores depend on student performance, the way the questions are asked, and other variables. These are all flows that impact and change a system. Stocks act as a current snapshot of the changing actions of the flows in a system.

On Diagram 1, you can see the illustration of how stocks and flows work. The big rectangle in the middle is the stock itself, in our case the school. There is an inflow affecting the stock, which In my example is the arriving students. The stock also experiences an outflow: students who leave, graduate, or dropout. But the inflow and outflow affecting the stock could be anything else: the inflow and outflow of school funds, the average success of the students taking tests, the teacher's motivation after changes in salary... any interconnection affects the school system.

Understanding the interactions and dynamics of stocks and flows, and their behaviors over time can help you to understand the behavior of the system as a whole.

Some systems don't have inflow. Let's look at the example of a newly found oil field. It took Mother Nature hundreds of thousands of years to create the oil reservoir under the ground. We can safely bet that if someone starts extracting the oil from this field, he will do it quicker than nature can replace it.

Diagram 2: Stock with one outflow.

Understanding Graphs

Systems thinkers are more interested in studying trends over time than individual events. Graphs are a tool they utilize to help make these trends visual. When you look at a graph that displays the behavior of a system over time, you can see if a system is close to reaching a goal or a limit and how quickly you might expect it to get there. The variable on a graph is often a stock or flow. When you look at a graph through a systems thinking lens, you want to be less concerned with exact numbers on the graph because they represent a snapshot of just a moment in time and individual events. It better serves you to look at the shape of the variable line as well as the places where the line changes shape or direction. Those are the representations of the trends and behaviors over time. The horizontal axis shows you the timeline of the trends happening in the system. Here you can see what happened before and forecast what might come next.

If you have ever lived with children, you know that they can accumulate quite the collection of toys. For the purpose of this example, picture a child having fifty toys. If you stop buying new toys for the child and she just keeps the toys she currently has, there will be no inflow or outflow and the number of toys the child has will stay exactly the same. This represents a stagnant system.

If you no longer purchase new toys and the child continuously breaks or donates some of her toys, the collection of toys will drop in number until eventually there aren't any toys left. (See Diagram 3.) In other words, there is only outflow on the stock. Let's say the child gives away five toys weekly. You can follow the trend of the decreasing stock by reviewing the graph of your child's behavior. Imagine you are standing at week four. By week four the child has "lost" twenty toys. Considering that the child has fifty toys, the total stock of the toys will be depleted in ten weeks.

But what if the child donates one toy at the same time she receives one new toy. What will happen to the toy collection now? The number of toys will stay constant at the current number because the inflow of new toys is now equal to the outflow of the old toys. One comes, one goes. The stock is now in a state of *dynamic equilibrium*. The level of the stock (toys) doesn't change even though there are continuous inflows and outflows through the system.

The example with the toy collection was the representation of a very simple system where there was only one stock, one inflow, and one outflow.

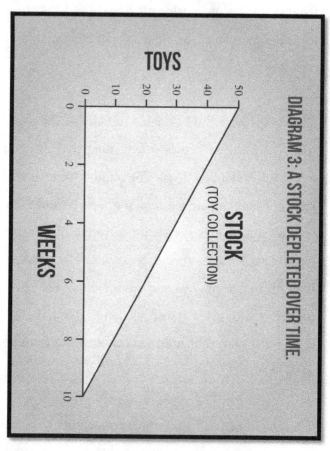

Diagram 3: A stock depleted over time.

There can be more inflows and outflows that affect the stock. On Diagram 4 you can see the stock affected by two inflows and outflows. Regardless of how many flows affect this stock, the following principles will hold true:

- If the sum of all of the inflows is greater than the sum of all of the outflows, the amount of the stock will increase.
- If the sum of all of the outflows is greater than the sum of all of the inflows, the amount of the stock will decrease.
- If the sum of all of the inflows and the sum of all of the outflows are equal, the amount of the stock will not change. It will remain in a state of dynamic equilibrium at whatever level it was at when the inflows and outflows became equal.

Diagram 4: A stock with multiple inflows and outflows.

DIAGRAM 4: A STOCK WITH MORE INFLOWS AND OUTFLOWS.

GIFTED TOYS

SELF-MADE TOYS

STOCK
(TOYS IN THE HOUSEHOLD)

BROKEN TOYS

DONATED TOYS

Our brains cause us to make common mistakes when it comes to stocks and flows. It is human nature for our brains to think more about stocks than flows. That means that in our example of our bank account, we pay more attention to the total amount of money we currently have than we do to the income or spending flowing into or out of it. When we do pay attention to flows, it is more natural for our brains to focus on the inflow rather than the outflow. This means that if we are not accumulating the amount of wealth that we want to, we are more likely to see the solution as needing to bring in more income when, in reality, it is possible to achieve the same result by decreasing our spending.

We can adjust the flows of our systems more quickly than we can the level of our stock. In our bank account example, we can immediately start to increase the amount of our income by taking a second job, or decreasing our spending right away by eating out less or buying cheaper things at the grocery store. But it will take some time to see the results in our bank account by having our stock level increase and accumulating a healthier bank balance.

It takes time for stocks to change because it takes time for flows to flow. Stocks tend to change more slowly (especially if they are large) because they react to change more gradually. This impacts the behavior of a system because there will inevitably be *a delay* between when a flow starts working and the level of the stock responds. It takes long time to populate a virgin soil with a forest. Even with the right incentives, years will pass until the population of a country shows growth or decay.

The delays and gaps in time before stocks react to change can cause problems for systems, but they can also serve as a stabilizing factor. For example, the more machines improve, the more human made workplaces they claim. However, these changes don't get implemented immediately or comprehensively. There is a delay between implementing a machine and replacing human labor with that machine. Thus, the worker can mentally prepare to the change to come and find a new job, or learn a new skill. Delays can also buy us time to observe and reflect on what is happening in the system's behavior and make changes to things that aren't working before it is too late and major damage has been done.

But you can approach the example of machines replacing humans from a different angle. Think of Charlie and the Chocolate Factory where Mr. Bucket had a miserable job putting the lids on toothpaste containers. At some point his job became automated by a machine. He got a better job fixing the machine that had replaced him when it broke down and he got paid a better wage because it was a more skilled position... You can look at the machine replacing humans case as an opportunity to learn a new skill and reenter the workforce in a new way that perhaps is more beneficial than an unskilled labor position. It never feels that way in the moment your job is being eliminated because you're panicking and trying to find a new job along with everyone else whose job was eliminated.

The existence of stocks makes it possible for flows to act independently of one another and to be out of balance with one another in the short term. The fact that you have savings in your account makes it possible for your spending to be unbalanced from your income for a limited period of time.

Most of our individual and system decisions are made because we want to control the level of our stock. In my house, if I run out of peppermint tea, it isn't long before I head to the store to buy more.

If the gas in your tank starts running low, you begin to look for the nearest gas station.

The decisions you make and actions you take are done with the goal of keeping the level of your stock within a favorable range. If you see the world in terms of being collections of stocks. You know you can control the levels of these stocks by adjusting the flows in a system. And now I will tell you exactly how you can adjust the flows: By utilizing "feedback processes."

Feedback Loops

Regardless of whether a stock level rises, drops, or simply remains constant over a period of time, we can safely conclude that there is a control mechanism in place controlling this behavior. Control mechanisms work through feedback loops.

A feedback loop happens when a stock's changes impacts its own inflows and outflows. For example, the amount of money in your bank account (stock) impacts how much interest you can earn from the account. The more money you have in your account, the more interest you will earn because the interest is calculated as a percentage of the total amount of money. If the amount of money you have in the bank (stock) drops, you will earn less interest. This is an example of a simple feedback loop where the change in the stock affects its own flows.[xv]

○ **Balancing Feedback Loops**

I have a friend who is diagnosed as being pre-diabetic. It is a warning sign that he needs to keep an eye on his intake of sugar and other lifestyle habits to keep it from advancing to diabetes. There are times during the day when his hands start to shake and he feels unstable. This is a sign to him that his blood sugar level is dropping too low and he might need to eat some food to help stabilize it. He knows how his body feels when his insulin level is within its normal range and he takes action throughout the day to keep it within that range. Whether it is shaking hands signaling to him to increase his blood sugar level, or his eyes suddenly becoming blurry signaling his sugar level is too high and indicating he should not eat any more sugary foods or simple carbohydrates, he makes decisions and takes action based on the feedback he gets from his body. The stock of blood sugar within his body is driven up or down from the flows of sugar and simple carbohydrates easily converted to glucose during digestion. (See Diagram 5 where B stands for balancing feedback loop.)

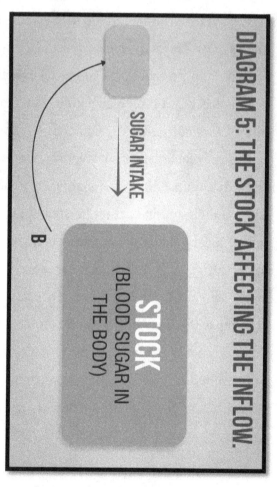

Diagram 5: A stock and a balancing feedback.

Balancing feedback loops seek stability and always have the goal of keeping stock levels within the range deemed acceptable. If a stock level rises too high, a balancing feedback loop will work to bring it back down where it should be. A balancing feedback loop will also work to increase a stock level if it has dropped too low.

Just because a feedback mechanism exists doesn't mean it's functioning well. Sometimes it simply isn't strong enough to overcome significant increases or decreases in stocks in order to return them to optimal levels.

The feedbacks stand for the interconnections in the system. As we learned earlier, interconnections hold essential information that a system needs in order to function, but they aren't infallible. Sometimes the information arrives too late or too early to be helpful. Sometimes it goes to the wrong person who doesn't understand its importance or how to best use it. Sometimes it may only be partial information or it might be misinterpreted. No matter the reason, sometimes the feedback loop may never actually get the stock to reach its target.

Reinforcing Feedback Loops

Another type of feedback loop is the reinforcing feedback loop. This loop magnifies and multiplies results, creating a cycle that can be hard to break free from. It can cause amazing growth or great harm.

Think of a reinforcing feedback loop as working in such a way that the rich get richer and the poor get poorer. When people have a lot of money or an excellent credit score, they are able to borrow money at the lowest interest rates, which they can then reinvest and use to make even more money. When people have a lower credit score or less money, they are forced to pay higher interest rates on their debt, which in turn costs them more money. More stock creates more inflow of additional stock while less stock creates a smaller inflow. Thus, income inequity between the upper class and middle and lower classes continues to widen.

Reinforcing feedback loops magnify whatever change is placed on them, causing the increases or decreases to be greater.

Here are a few examples:

- o When animals become endangered, there are less parents left to produce offspring, which means that the numbers can't grow and improve at a great enough rate to remove them from the endangered species list.

- When people earn more money, they make more purchases. When people are purchasing more goods, demand is high and the supply is low. This causes merchants to be able to charge more for their products (this also helps them to pay their employees more wages as well). As a result, people need to continue to earn more wages in order to be able to purchase goods at the same rate.

- The more rain that falls, the more standing water there is. The standing water is a breeding ground for mosquitos so, as a result, the mosquitos are able to reproduce at more rapid rates.

- When a child calls another child names, that child typically responds by calling names in return. The negative exchange usually escalates and continues between the children until someone steps in to intervene.

o When an athlete practices, they become more skilled in their sport. When they are better at their sport, they tend to enjoy it more. According to positive psychology, one naturally enjoys activities he is already naturally good at. Both cases lead the athlete to want to spend more time being active in his sport which serves as additional practice and further improves his skills.

Reinforcing feedback loops are self-supporting and can multiply very quickly. This means they have the potential to cause great growth and success or great harm. These loops exist anytime a stock has the ability to adjust its own level. Diagram 6 presents the reinforcing feedback loop (where R stands for reinforcing feedback) of reproducing rabbits in places where their natural predators decrease. The more rabbits that survive, the more will be able to produce offspring. If there is no human intervention and no increase in predators, the growth of the rabbit population won't stop. In this case, the only barrier to their growth would be the food available and the fighting between the male rabbits in the warren. But right now, let's just focus on the variables presented on the diagram.

If you have already begun to think of any feedback loops that you encounter in your daily life, you are well on your way to becoming a systems thinker. When you start thinking in systems you stop looking for scapegoats, but rather want to understand and examine the system as a whole.

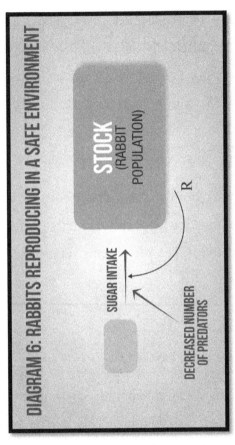

Diagram 6: A stock and a reinforcing feedback.

You will see that the behaviors and interconnections of a system, over time, can act differently than expected. They also can affect each other differently than expected. For example, you can notice that not only X has an impact on Y, but also Y can reflect back on X through a feedback mechanism. Systems are dynamic and cause their own behavior through feedback loops.

Before we go on to learn about how we can use systems thinking in practice, let's differentiate between two types of systems: open and closed systems.

Open and closed systems

If one thing is certain about living things, it is that they are always changing. This is true from the tiniest cells all the way up to the organism as a whole. The state of constant change contributes to organisms being open systems. An open system is one in which materials are entering and leaving it.

The inflow and outflow of materials serve to perpetually change the system because the individual elements within the system are also constantly being changed.

Closed systems are characterized as systems in which materials are not entering or leaving.

Basic biological phenomena are considered as being open systems. Examples of some open systems in the biological realm can include: metabolism, form development, growth, or digestion. Basically anything that has a cell and therefore relies on osmosis.

In a closed system, interactions only happen within the system. We can say closed systems are shut off from the outside environment, and every interaction is happening inside that closed system. This type of system has clear procedures that are not affected by external stimuli. A closed system is a system that exchanges only energy with its surroundings, not matter. Putting strawberries in a freezer is a closed system because freezers are airtight so matter can no longer transfer. The door prevents matter from entering and leaving the freezer. When variations in time disappear, the closed systems become stationary. They attain a state of equilibrium where the system composition remains constant. Closed systems must eventually reach a state of equilibrium, according to the second law of thermodynamics.[4] [xvi]

Open systems can attain a stationary condition. This happens when an open system appears constant, even though inflow and outflow are still happening. The levels are just remaining balanced and equal so the system is steady, even though materials are moving in and out of the system at the same rate.

---

[4] The second law of thermodynamics states that the total entropy of an isolated system can never decrease over time. The total entropy can remain constant in ideal cases where the system is in a steady state (equilibrium), or is undergoing a reversible process. From https://en.wikipedia.org/wiki/Second_law_of_thermodynamics

Chapter 4: Mental Models

What are mental models?

Whether it was a model of the solar system you saw in astronomy books, the model of an airplane or car you built as a hobby, or a computer simulation that shows a model of something complicated you use at work, chances are you have been exposed to models in some form in your life. What are models? Models take a complex system and simplify it, making it easier to understand. They are the abstract or simplified representation of something larger.

Are models the perfect mirror of what they aim to represent? No. Models usually present only a part of the complex system we wish to analyze. They crop a piece of reality out of the whole system so we can study it up close and learn from it. When creating a model we don't add every variable and influencer of a situation on purpose; taking every aspect into consideration would hardly make a complicated matter digestible. Thus, models should never be considered the final reality, but rather a tool that gets us closer to seeing and understanding the real objective of a complex system. Models are helpful learning tools.

Mental models are created within the mind. They are cognitive tools. In order to create a useful mental model, you need to be conscious and aware of the world around you and how you fit into it. What do I mean by this?

Imagine that you walk out in your back yard and see a rabbit sitting there. What happens? Your eyes (and sometimes other sensory organs) focus on and physically receive the image of the rabbit and send messages about it to your brain. In the initial split second that you see the rabbit, you don't know what you're actually seeing. You're just receiving visual information. It isn't until the visual information reaches your brain that the understanding of the rabbit deepens. The rabbit is a concept of your external reality. But you wouldn't understand what you're seeing is a rabbit if you've never seen a rabbit before or you didn't know what a rabbit looks like.

The information from your eyes or other sensory organs are not enough on their own to create understanding. Part of what it takes to acknowledge what the rabbit is, as a concept, comes from past experiences and prior knowledge. Your knowledge and experience surrounding the concept of a rabbit creates your mental models about it.

If you know the same rabbits I do, we can agree that the rabbit is a mammal known for its strong sense of hearing and quickness, which helps it to escape from predators. Depending on the type of rabbit and where it lives, its fur color may change with the seasons in order to help it use camouflage and blend in more with its surroundings for protection. It is an herbivore, which means it eats plants. It breathes in oxygen and exhales carbon dioxide. Thanks to the mental model I have in my brain about rabbits, I can be confident about the fact that rabbits won't attack me, and I need not be alarmed or fearful when looking at a rabbit. I can conclude that I'm safe if a rabbit is in my back yard. I state this with a strong belief based on my past experiences with and prior knowledge of rabbits.

Mental models are made up of knowledge that we already have and help us to add new knowledge to it.

In a simple system model, like a causal loop diagram, the elements in action are linked in a cause and effect relationship. Sometimes, however, we can't clearly understand the thought processes behind these connections. How does investing in leadership development result in less employee turnover? How can a change in communication style lead to an improved relationship? How does a gesture of kindness change the opinion of our rivals?

Understanding the mental models behind these cause and effect connections help better understand the mechanisms responsible for creating a certain behavior. It can also help us to come up with better solutions to problems.

Adding our observations of the thought processes by mapping our mental models to the causal loop diagram helps go beyond a superficial understanding and see things we might otherwise miss. We call this step Going Deeper™.

How do we "go deeper?" First, we need to design a causal loop diagram for a system-level problem. (See an example of a causal loop diagram in Diagram 7.) Second, we need to look at our completed diagram and search for links that result from human decisions. For example, a headline such as "the change in state support negatively affected the budget for health care" is a mathematical reality. The less money an institution receives, the less it will have to distribute. However, if we take a look at the decision makers behind the new health care policies, we can see the human involvement.

When we find a connection point that was due to human decision, we need to ask this question: Why is this decision being made? It is important to try to get into the mindset and perspective of the person or people responsible for making the choice. Once you feel like you have an understanding of their perspective, add it to the map as a visual representation by drawing a thought bubble above the human choice connection.

Types of Mental Models

Predictions and guesses

When we use mental models, our minds are automatically jumping to conclusions of what will come next. Let's play a game. I'll show you a picture of a dog jumping for a ball. What are your thoughts of this picture? Did you just imagine the dog catching the ball? Or rather you imagined it missing the ball and falling back to the ground while the ball rolls far away? Regardless of what you imagined, you were actively –but unconsciously - using your mental models. You can't know what happens next in a static picture. Thus your imagination is a prediction or guess. Multiple conclusion scenarios are possible. Using mental models primes our brains to think ahead to possible future outcomes and consequences.

The Theory of Constraints[xvii]

If you've ever heard the phrase "a team is only as strong as its weakest link," then you have an understanding of this type of mental model. The Theory of Constraints[xviii] recognizes that every system is limited by constraints, and by nature, there will always be one constraint that exerts more pressure on a system than all of the others. This constraint becomes the bottleneck that causes the biggest problem in the system.

Since, like a team, a system can only perform as well as its weakest link, an emerging bottleneck issue will negatively impact the performance of the entire system. The system, as a whole, will not improve unless the bottleneck is resolved.

We can take this idea to our own personal goals for improvement. If we don't figure out the real source of what is holding us back and slowing us down, our own bottleneck you might say, we will just continue to run in circles and not reach our goals and live our best life. We may make some changes in our life and even feel like we are moving forward, but if the bottleneck isn't addressed, we will, in essence, be stuck in the same place. It isn't necessary for us to work harder. We just need to work smarter and make needed changes in the area of maximum impact. For example, we can buy better photo editing software, but if we fail to understand the needs of the market we want target or, there will be no improvement in our sales.

Removing a bottleneck is not the end of our journey. We will always be a work in progress. We have to remove our current bottleneck so we can move on with our improvement project. We can have secondary challenges, but they will not be solved unless we get a grip on our primary challenge. We can't improve our system and move forward until we address the real problem holding us back. Our bottleneck needs our primary focus until we can correct it. Only then will we really be ready to move on. When we overcome a bottleneck issue, the entire system will go through a changing phase; it will readjust to the new circumstances.

Use mind mapping to identify bottlenecks. Remember, first design a causal loop diagram, and then identify human decisions among the links. Ask "Why is this decision being made?" Answer it. Then analyze if this decision is prolonging, triggering, or reinforcing the existence of the problem or not. Dig deeper if you've confirmed that the decision is a possible catalyst for the problem. How? By trying to find the catalyst of your catalyst. I know, I'm spiraling out of the easy-to-follow category. Let me present bottleneck mind mapping through the example of trying to lose weight.

Let's imagine a man who has wanted to lose a few pounds for a long time, thinking that he'll become happier if he's twenty pounds lighter. He worked out constantly, but he also ate snacks mindlessly whenever he sat down to watch television at night. Thus he experienced no major improvements. The human decision in this case is binge eating in front of the TV. "Why is this decision being made?" Because the person in question has eaten mindlessly. Or because he is addicted to sugar. Research studies have shown that sugar is more addicting in lab rats than cocaine, yet we pour sugar in our coffee, in our soda, in our tea, everything. Some people are growing up not knowing how to eat properly. Perhaps he rationalizes that just because he burned 500 calories in the gym he can now he can eat 400 calories in chocolate and he'd still be 100 calories in the negative. This is not how diets work, and he knows this. Why isn't he respecting the diet more–especially after putting so much effort into his goal at the gym? This is a question that can be answered using psychology. The lack of self-control and the purposeful self-sabotage can both be rooted in low self-respect and a lack of self-love. If someone doesn't consider himself or his goals worthy of effort, he usually has a negative self-image and bad habits related to it.

While at the beginning of the analysis it may have seemed that binging was the bottleneck problem of this man, after digging deeper, we've discovered that other issues might be the real causes of the unsuccessful diet and binging was rather just another effect of a more profoundly rooted cause.

If he gave up on binging at one point and achieved his goal of weight loss, he'd probably still be unhappy with himself because he didn't fix his bottleneck problem: the lack of self-acceptance and self-love. He'd torment himself with another inadequacy he identified within, even if that meant returning to his old eating habits and regaining the weight he'd worked so hard to lose. Either way, he'd just reinforce his negative self-image.

With the help of a mental model, this man could identify his bottleneck problem and exercise effort in changing it. If he becomes more accepting and kind with himself, he'll lose the weight because he wishes to nurture his body by staying healthy. He will stick to his diet for the same reasons. Thus, he'll reach his goal of weight loss and satisfaction.

Feedback Loop Installation[xix]

We discussed feedback loops in the last chapter. We have balancing feedback loops that work to maintain equilibrium and reinforcing feedback loops which can either cause growth or decline to a system.

People implant balancing feedback loops in systems when they want to keep it steady and consistent. They protect themselves from force majeure events rocking the boat and having a negative impact on the system. These pre-implanted balancing feedback loops are checkpoints that can reduce the damage of a negative event and give people time and opportunity for reflection to decide the next best step. Thus, they can evaluate whether things are progressing as they had hoped and continue on the same course, or whether they need additional help or a new plan of action.

This being said, we need to stay aware of the counterbalancing feedback loops around us as well. What goes around comes back around, the saying goes. There are cases when a balancing feedback loop, originally meant to balance the system, overflows, and to keep the equilibrium, some other forces start to take action in order to maintain the status quo. For example, we want to save a fixed amount, let's say $100, every month. If we start spending more on hobbies to enhance our life quality, we'll need to cut spending in other areas, like our essentials, or we can aim to earn more so we need to work overtime or take a second part-time job. To balance the loop of hobbies, the counterbalancing loop of cutting expenses on essentials or working overtime steps in. (Of course, assuming that we'll stick to our $100 saving plan no matter what.)

This example may seem irrelevant, but put this idea on a larger scale. The government needs to maintain a state budget that can't decrease under a certain level, otherwise the state will go bankrupt. Normally in this type of situation there would be a mandatory percentage budget cut and all state agencies would have to do them. A lot of times any vacant positions are eliminated to cover the costs, for example. But if this rectification is not enough and they want to give tax cuts, they need to tighten their belts in other areas; they can no longer distribute as much as they had in previous years for education, health, or research and development. Conversely, if the government wishes to dispense more money to R&D and education, it needs to collect more in taxes to keep the fragile balance of the state budget.

Reinforcing feedback loops are implanted when we want to continually set higher standards for our system. These loops are helpful when we want to assure our growth over time. "The journey of a thousand miles begins with a single step" and it finishes only if we make all the next steps, slowly but steadily walking the finish line. If we want to achieve long term lasting growth, we have to start with small steps and continue to build on them day after day. These small efforts will result in exponential growth.

For example, depositing our $100 savings month by month on our savings account will result in the exponential growth of our savings portfolio.

The Borrowing Example

Our minds have an easier time understanding our own realities. We can easily create mental models of things that are tangible, simple, and recent. Mental models become more challenging when the things we analyze are more abstract or removed from our personal experience. The Systems thinker [xx] takes a closer look at the example of borrowing money to bring an abstract concept into a more concrete mental model. They present the situation of a couple who had to make purchases on their credit cards because of a series of events that required money and a shortage of readily available cash. Over time, the high rate of interest on the credit cards caused an even more shortage of cash. To create a mental model that gives a profound insight to the couple's situation, follow the following five steps created by The Systems Thinker:

1. Draw a causal loop diagram:
   In the beginning, borrowing money will seem like a good solution to a shortage of readily available funds. When you borrow money you have access to more cash, but this will only be true in the short-term. (B1 – As you borrow money, the cash shortage

temporarily decreases.) As time goes on, high interest payments will reduce the amount of money you have. (R1) This solution ultimately proves to be unsuccessful.

2. Add a thought bubble to any link where human choice was involved.

   The "human choice" in this example is made by the person who has made the conscious decision to borrow money. Add this choice to the arrow connecting "Cash Flow Problems" and "Borrowing."

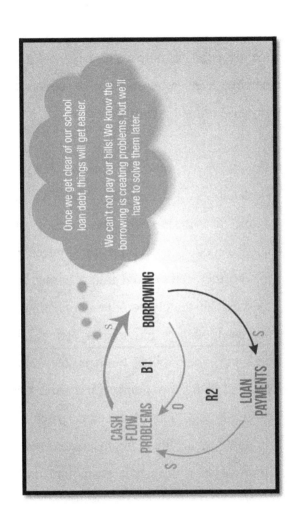

Diagram 7: The case of borrowing[xxi]

3. Assume the borrower thinks rationally. Ask yourself "why did the borrower make the decision to borrow money, and then borrow even more money to cover the expense of his first borrowing?"

4. Try to come up with several possible explanations. Perhaps they were worried about "keeping up with the Joneses" and needed money to keep up appearances. Or maybe they felt backed into a corner like they had absolutely no other choice than to borrow money to provide for their family and pay their bills. Perhaps they only planned to borrow money for a short time to get through a rough financial patch and thought their life circumstances would improve soon through a promotion, raise, or new job that did not materialize.

5. Try to see the situation from more perspectives. Try to understand the reason and emotions for their choice. The more you are able to come up with a variety of reasons for the different people involved in making the decision they did, the more complete picture you will have of the situation.[xxii]

By Going Deeper™ , we are able to learn a lot more about the system and why it behaves the way it does. If we only looked at superficial aspects of the system, we would miss out on the hidden reasons that come with the deeper analysis of the family system. Jumping to simple conclusions and finding someone or something to blame for problems that have occurred within the system, we wouldn't be able to learn valuable information to take with us and apply it in the future.

Going even deeper

It's not enough to be content to simply try and understand a system. The ultimate goal is to use the deeper understanding we've gained to take action and change the system for the better.

We have already discussed making the causal loop diagram and using mental models, but Richard Karash and Michael Goodman take this process a few steps further as explained in their article *Going Deeper: Moving from Understanding to Action.*[xxiii] Here are the next four steps they advise aspiring systems thinkers to take into consideration:

1. Explore the Purpose
    Ask yourself where you are now and where you hope to be. It is only by taking a hard, honest look at your current reality, of where you are at the present time as well as what your true goals of a successful outcome from the

system would look like that you can begin to close the gap and achieve your vision.

2. Examine Mental Models
   Go deeper than the superficial layer of a system. Assume that everyone involved is acting rationally and try to get to the bottom of understanding why they might have made the decisions they did. These ideas should get added to the causal loop diagrams as thought bubbles.

3. Acknowledge Personal Responsibility
   It is human nature to want to place blame outside of ourselves when things go wrong. That's how we're wired. The problem with that line of thinking, though, is that it also gives away our power. If we refuse to accept the role

we might play in the current problems the system is having, we also give away our ability to be a part of a real and lasting solution. Systems thinkers aren't looking to place blame; they are looking for solutions. Very often positive change begins with us.

4. Expand the View

Problems in systems rarely occur in a vacuum. They have connections to both the past and the future. We just have to be willing to look for them. It is equally important to know if the system has ever been in the same situation before as it is to know what your vision is for success on the other side. Learning from the past and creating a bridge to the future is important in improving a system. Try to consider all possible consequences before creating an action plan, and then start moving forward.

Chapter 5: Systems Essentials

Systems of all types that are high functioning have three characteristics in common: they are resilient, self-organizing, or they are a thriving hierarchy.

Resilience

Systems are pushed and stretched - often to their limits. Their long-term success will be measured by their ability to bounce back and recover from challenges and adversity in a timely manner. Adaptability and elasticity are the keywords.

Systems have a variety of feedback loops in place, working in different ways to help the system recover when it strays off its path and away from achieving its purpose or function. Resilience isn't an easily recognizable characteristic of a system, especially if we don't look at the system as a whole. For example, if we only examine a broken bone within the first three days of the incident, we might conclude that the human body is not resilient. Fell off the monkey bars and broke my arm. However, if we look at the same broken bone a year later, we can see how resilient our body really is, recovering from the break completely in nearly all cases. When we look at the big picture of the system as a whole, we can really confirm its resilience.

There are cases when systems lose their resilience. Take your own body, for example. It is exposed to many viruses and bacteria each day without you being aware of it. If your body, your immune system is healthy, it will fight back against these invaders and stay healthy; you might catch a cold depending on the germ attacking your immune system, but you'll heal eventually. Some diseases, however, don't get cured over time. AIDS, Multiple Sclerosis, or some stages of cancer would be a good example of loss of immune system resilience.

Resilience can be lost with aging. This is especially true in the case of living systems. Think about bone density depleting over a woman's lifetime. Due to the brittleness of her bones the hip breaks and then due to that same brittleness the recovery is longer and more arduous than with a younger person and so she gets more laid up and her health declines because she doesn't exercise regularly or eat as well because standing to cook is a strain. This woman would need not only the help of an orthopedist but also probably a highly skilled internist who would look at her nutritional health, be the point person for organizing her hip recovery and therapy, but also help manage her mental health through this difficult recovery. An injury like this could devastate who had been an otherwise vibrant person and would be a more profound breakdown of multiple sub-systems in her body.

Some disasters happen because of human involvement. Ford Motor Company and its dumping of toxic sludge on or near lands for the Ramapough Mountain Indians contaminated the soil, air and groundwater of the community for a long time. The Ramapough Mountain Tribe and other residents of Ringwood, New Jersey sued Ford Motor Company and other defendants for property damage. (Wayne Mann, et al. v. Ford Motor Company, et al. case)[xxiv]

Due to rapidly changing weather conditions that were caused in part by wastewater treatment ponds and in part from smoke stacks from the Bowater Paper Mill there was a 100 car pileup among a three mile stretch of I-75 in Tennessee that resulted in thirteen fatalities and forty-two injuries. This stretch of road was already notoriously dangerous for sudden, blindingly thick fog, and after this accident the Tennessee

Department of Transportation implemented more measures to help drivers see and closing access to the highway once fog reached a specific density, but even Bowater's own report analysts stated that the smoke stacks prevented the water vapor rising off the waste water ponds being evaporated and was creating this deadly fog that was partially responsible for the accidents.[xxv]

Some species go extinct due to changed environmental conditions, and they lose their resilience and adaptability because the change is too extreme to withstand. Other species overpopulate because they don't have any natural predator anymore. The use of certain pesticides in the farming industry temporarily solved the problem of crop munching insects, but just as these insects disappeared, other insect populations rose to power, which were more resilient, and the old pesticides were not effective on them. Using stronger, or different pesticides would have not helped in long term either. While some species would always become dominant, the soil would get saturated with poison in a chemical war against the insects.[xxvi]

There were attempts to break the pesticide vicious circle by introducing new, natural predators to farms. This method has been largely unsuccessful outside of the animals' natural ecosystem. In Australia, they purposely introduced the cane toad to prey on a specific beetle that disrupted sugar cane production. Toads did their "job" well but they also had no natural predators. These toads are poisonous to the touch as they carry toxin in their skin. Since Australian predators aren't adapted to the toxin, they may kill the frog, but it often costs them their lives. The cane toads are prolific breeders and all attempts to manage or curb them have failed.[xxvii]

We've seen similar issues in the Everglades, Florida with two apex predators: alligators and errantly introduced pythons by wayward owners wanting to get rid of a constrictor that has gotten too big, expensive, or is just no longer wanted. Instead of properly rehoming the animal in another terrarium, which takes time to find, owners were just releasing them in masse in the wild where they are now breading uncontrollably in a very hidden environment.[xxviii]

Each change we make in a system has an effect on its resilience. That is why it is important to examine and predict how a system would react to our interventions from many angles and try to predict every possible outcome and consequence before taking action.

Although sometimes something sounds appealing in the short-term, we don't really want to sacrifice a system's resilience and make it more dependent on human involvement. Our ultimate goal should be to ensure that systems can persevere through adversity with as little unnatural input as possible.

You have likely heard the Chinese proverb that wisely states "Give a man a fish and you feed him for a day. Teach a man to fish and you feed him for a lifetime." This is true of systems as well. We want them to be able to function on their own as independently as possible. We should aim to boost a systems' self-restorative ability. In case of the pesticide-insect issue, instead of intervening chemically, natural ecosystems should be promoted. The predators of the insects we wish to get rid of should be allowed to handle the pests, and sustainable farming techniques that retain soil quality over the long-term should be practiced over techniques that pillage the soil of all its riches in a few short years. This way the balance of nature wouldn't be disturbed and the soil quality wouldn't degrade either.[xxix]

Self-organization

Another characteristic of well-functioning systems is self-organization. Think about how the first communities, tribes, city-states, and, later, nation-states evolved out of formerly scattered humans. People learned to live in communities, evolved and diversified their skills, and as their community became more complex, they were able to come up with laws and guidelines to keep this complexity in relative order.

Self-organization is a valuable ability, but it is so general in living systems that we hardly take it into consideration. Unfortunately, many times we are oblivious to the evolvement of self-organization that takes place in front of us. We fail to aid it, or worse, we perpetually work against it.

For example, think about when we overdose ourselves with caffeine to stay awake when our body is on the brink of exhaustion. We may influence our body's processes on the short-term, but long-term interference backfires. If we don't get enough rest in at time and artificially boost ourselves with stimulants, the body will turn against itself and shut down our system in a way no amount of caffeine can resurrect.

Giving too many instructions and overly strict evaluations can kill employees' creativity and morale. Relying too much to old rules may give one a sense of control and stability, but in the long run it banishes innovation and optimization.

Supporting self-organization in a system requires a loosening of the reins and being willing to let go of a bit of control to give the system the chance and freedom to do what comes naturally. It means letting go and allowing a degree of trial and error within the system. This is often difficult as things can become messy at times and it can be hard for people to adopt a hands-off policy long enough to let the self-organization work fully. It's a little like wanting to let your kids use paint and glitter for an art project or help cook in the kitchen, but being terrified of the mess that they'll make. Sometimes we intervene because we can't help ourselves.

Luckily, no constraint lasts forever. Even from underneath the heaviest stone-built temples of Cambodia, trees and vegetation found a way to break up to the surface. After the bloodiest wars and deadliest diseases, the nations affected have found a way to move on, re-organize themselves, adapt to the new circumstances and rebuild, and some have even thrived. The aforementioned Cambodia is a good example of this Phoenix-like resurrection. Under the terroristic rules of the Khmer Rouge 1.5 to 3 million people died, it was known as Cambodia's Killing Fields.[xxx] Some holy places were filled up with the dead bodies of innocent casualties. Yet, after the horror was over, the people of Cambodia buried and properly mourned their dead, cleaned the holy places, and today, together, in unity they pray for a better future.

This being said, it's important to add that not all nations thrive after a difficult period. Free nations usually thrive, but nations that are very corrupt are often corrupt at the expense of their people. (Even the free nations take advantage of corruption and the regular citizens' gullibility.)

The Democratic Republic of Congo is one of the richest countries in the world in terms of natural resources. It has the minerals that our cell phones, computers, and gaming systems cannot be made without and they are only found here.[xxxi] There is a copper belt here, but a lot of the Congolese people don't have running water in their homes, child labor is a very real part of life there. The men are ill equipped for the heavy duty mining they do, often wearing cheap Wellington boots-like footwear not thick soled, steel toed work boots. It is almost mind-blowing that every single person in that country is not wealthy and they aren't because of the corruption involved with selling the contracts to mine that land of those minerals.

A student send an email once for a fellow teacher from the Democratic Republic of Congo asking she I'd give him a waiver for a required standardized test because the only testing center was in the most northwestern corner of the country and he lived in the most southeastern corner of the country and travel conditions were unsafe and somewhat lethal. We verified, and what the student said was all true and accurate. After checking this place on Google Earth) we were agreeing that we wouldn't ask anyone to risk their life for a test score.

Thus I can conclude that the self-organization quality of a system, while is extremely valuable, it can turn into a negative angle.

Hierarchy

Systems can be divided into smaller subsystems. For example, in a forest ecosystem you have all of the living things. You can break this down into the subsystems of plants and animals. If you look at the animals, you can further divide them into smaller subsystems like mammals, birds, reptiles, amphibians, and insects.

Taking just one of those subsystems, mammals, you could break it down into animals like squirrels, bears, rabbits, and deer among others. If we look at one individual mammal within the taxonomic index you will find it has a kingdom, genus, and species, all which narrows in greater and greater detail about the animal, plant, bacteria, protozoa, etc. indexed. This is a system hierarchy in action.[xxxii]

Living systems are not the only kind of system that utilizes hierarchies. You find this type of organization in corporations, military, financial institutions, government, education, and so many others. Why? Because it works. Organization through hierarchy can serve as a stabilizing force in a system and can lead to greater efficiency and productivity. In 2013 Croatia joined the European Union, becoming the 28th member of the organization. The EU thus consists of 28 countries, each having their own governments. These governments consist of a prime minister and/or a president, ministers, and local governments. These subsystems are all working individually, but they depend on the larger systems above them to meet the desired goals of the union.

Living things are perfectly designed by nature to exist through the hierarchy of systems and subsystems. Let's look at a mammal, for example. Cells survive and multiply on their own. That subsystem works together to make and support tissues, which in turn work together to make and support organs. Those organs work together to make and support organs and systems such as the gastrointestinal system, cardiothoracic system, or neurological system. Those organs, systems, and all of the other subsystems work together to create and support an organism. Then the organism is part of a larger species living together. Those species are part of a larger ecosystem living and working together. These smaller subsystems, even down to the smallest cells, can, by and large, take care of and support themselves. They also work together to help meet the needs of the larger subsystems and overarching system above them in the hierarchy at the same time. The dominant system acts a bit like the conductor of an orchestra. It ensures that the subsystems work together and that their functions coordinate to make the system a strong, stable, successful, resilient, and well-functioning one.

All of the subsystems are connected within the system, but each individual subsystem has its closest connections within. Think about it like the people at a baseball game. The players, coaches, umpires, fans, ushers, concession employees, announcers, grounds crew, parking attendants, security guards, ticket takers, and others are all part of the baseball game system. They all work together to create the experience and atmosphere of the game. Each subsystem is responsible for a specific purpose within the overarching system. Even though they are all connected to each other, the strength of those connections is not equal between all of them. The players, coaches, and fans of team A will be much closer and more connected to each other than they will be to any of the other subsystems, especially those who are a part of team B. But even in the sub-system of team A, the players will be more connected to each other than they are to their fans, right? The members of the grounds crew will be more strongly connected to each other than they would be to the concession employees because they work more closely with each other and spend more time together.

Hierarchies evolve bottom up, from part to whole. The foundational guiding purpose of a hierarchy is to help the smaller subsystems function better and have the support they need. This is turn serves the system as a whole, because if the little parts do their jobs better, the entire system will benefit and perform more efficiently. In many cases the levels of the hierarchy forget that they need to work together and aim to achieve everyone's goals, and that's why they're so badly functioning hierarchies and the system's goals aren't met.

When subsystems think of their purpose as being more important than that of the system, and achieving their goals comes at the expense of and detriment to the entire system, the process is called sub-optimization. On the other hand, if the top levels of the hierarchy control and stifle the lower levels to the extent that they are prevented from carrying out their functions, the system as a whole will suffer the same as in cases of sub-optimization.

To a degree, a highly functioning system is a lot like a democracy. In the United States, the freedoms and rights of individual citizens and laws in individual states are protected and encouraged even if they undermine the federal law. Many states have, in the past few years, legalized medical and recreational marijuana usage. Marijuana usage is still federally illegal.

You can transport weed over state lines, but the states retain more power to self govern than the federal government.

The central guiding force that the entire government system must follow is the United States Constitution, but the freedoms afforded to the representatives from the House and Senate and how these sub-systems work to pass laws or represent their constituents in Washington. While the US has a relatively powerful federal government, the real power has always been with the states. The power of the Federal government only is allowed to do what is expressed in the constitution (which is a living breathing document - it changes) or what it has usurped and not been called out on.

Event Level Vs. Behavior Level Analysis

When we talk of a system's behavior, we look at how it performs over time. Has it grown, stayed the same, or declined? Is it well-organized or random? How has it evolved and changed?

If you love reading about history, you know that having retrospective data on a given historical event made the outcome quite predictable. Surely, not so much for the people who lived in that historical period, but for us, readers and historical analysts of today. Let's take the Roman Empire as an example. While the central authority was strong and united, the empire was invincible, operating with an organizational system that could keep its tens of millions of subjects under control. The empire was facing external threats, attacks by the Goths in the north and of the Parthians in the south, but they overcame adversities and thrived. It wasn't until the death of Emperor Commodus in 192 AD and the death of the Antoninus Dynasty that the empire started to decline, slowly but surely.[xxxiii] Since Commodus had no heirs hadn't appointed anyone to take his place, chaos and individual greed started to overtake the goal of the system as a whole, namely to keep together and enrich the Roman Empire. One hundred and eighty-four years after the death of Commodus, in 476 AD, the Roman Empire collapsed.

The collapse of a great empire is not unique. Before the Romans, there was the Macedonian Empire of Alexander the Great, which suffered the same fate. Centuries later the Napoleon's First French Empire ended up sharing the experience of the Romans. The common feature in all these stories is that while subsystems were working toward the benefit of the system as a whole and the system provided the subsystems their needs, these great empires were undefeatable. When this balance changed, the empire-systems collapsed. An interesting exception that empowers the rule of "all empires must collapse" is the British recovery from the loss of all their colonies. While the British Empire collapsed, their home base remained independent and not taken over by an external invader. The British colonial empire doesn't exist anymore, yet Britain didn't wither and die. It's still a strong and powerful nation. It thrived in a new and different way while also having to manage the loss its colonies – and all those colonies provided.

Looking at the timeline of the Roman Empire, or the empire of Alexander the Great, we can clearly detect the rise, the peak, and the downfall of each of them. But what would happen if we only looked at Commodus' death, or a single successful conquest of Alexander? Could we predict or have a clear picture on the empire's behavior just by losing our minds on this –once- breaking news? Not really, right?

When we study specific individual events superficially as if they happened in isolation we won't get answers to questions like "what now?" or "what will happen to the country?" or "how will this event affect the economy?" Just like in history, in our modern age we don't get accurate information just by putting one event under the microscope. To get the answers we seek, we need to dig deeper and make a behavior over time analysis.

Systems thinkers automatically look for data and history when they are presented with a problem. They want to know if the system has ever been in the same position before. They begin to study the data and look for patterns over time. Studying long-term behavior is a window into the underlying structure within the system and it can reveal a wealth of information about what is happening in it, and more importantly, why it's happening. It is only then that we can get to the heart of a problem and uncover a possible improvement.

A system's structure is formed by its stocks, flows, and feedback loops. The structure is made visible through causal loop diagrams, complete with boxes, arrows, and thought bubbles. The structure of such diagrams will show what behavior tendencies a system has. As I mentioned before, when we encounter a balancing feedback loop, we can conclude that the system is working toward maintaining or establishing a dynamic equilibrium while a reinforcing feedback loop indicates exponential growth or decline. The two main indicators that systems thinkers use are time graphs and diagrams of the stock, flows, and feedback.

Football games are a good example of event level analysis. Perhaps you have heard of Monday Morning Quarterbacks. They are the people who are eager to offer their opinions and commentary, usually quite critically, on the performance of a player or team in a football game that occurred over the previous weekend. They do not hesitate to judge and criticize the performance of others once the game has happened. They can usually be found complaining to their friends or calling into radio shows offering their opinions and criticism with little basis in long established facts or any attempt to dig deeper and study the history behind the performance. While this analysis may be entertaining, it is more superficial and does little to help us predict what will happen in future games.

However, I must add in MMQ's defense that a lot of this information is top secret. The NE Patriots aren't going to be releasing videos of their practice drills to the general public because they don't want other teams prepping to their strategies. The other team only gets previous game play videos to strategize with. Meanwhile each team takes extensive video of their practice drills and they breakdown each play and analyze it to death so each member of the team knows their part backward and forward and it hopefully goes off seamlessly and without an injury.

On the other hand, coaches, medical staff, sideline reporters, and seasoned analysts of the game would make every effort to look for long-term behavior and patterns as an explanation for the player or team's performance. They would look at injury reports, study game tape - both current and from the past, conduct interviews, and study data in the form of statistics to assess whether the team had been in the same or a similar position before and try to get a more complete picture and explanation of the reasons behind the performance.

This type of behavior level analysis by being connected to both the present and the past as well as based on hard data, gives us a better picture of performance over time, and makes us more likely to anticipate to a degree what might lie ahead for the team.

The nonlinear world

Much to the chagrin of our linear-thinking minds, we live in a nonlinear world. Systems often surprise us when they react and perform in nonlinear ways. In the realm of linear thinking an action will have a consequence – small action small consequence, big action big consequence. This isn't always the case in nonlinear systems. You may think that if you add a small stimulus or push in a system, you will get a small response in return, and if you triple that response, you except to see a response that is three times as strong. The reality is that same-level response is just one possibility among many. The response may also just as easily be far greater or far less than we expect based on the stimulus applied.

Here's one example: when the election season is upon us, the candidates running for office in both parties begin to roll out their advertisements to convince voters to support them in the election. They send flyers through the mail, place signs on billboards and in yards throughout their campaign area, hold rallies, send representatives door-to-door to speak on their behalf, make phone calls to people within their political party, increase their social media presence, and run commercials on television and radio stations. While some advertising can be good for making potential voters aware of them and their message, and possibly increase the number of votes they receive, it is also possible that too much advertising may have the opposite effect and cause voters to become annoyed and tune out their message making them less likely to vote for them in the election.

Or consider an avalanche. Avalanches "need" three parts to happen: snow, a sloped surface and a trigger. A weak layer within the snowpack, caused by ice, surface or depth hoar, if meeting a trigger such as a minimal amount of fresh snow or a little motion, can release a cascade of destructive snow down the side of a mountain.

Nonlinearities confuse us because they challenge and often prove wrong our expectations regarding what type of response we will get from taking a particular action. This is not the only purpose they serve. Nonlinearities are capable of causing the entire behavior of a system to flip and change course because they change the relative strength of feedback loops.

When you see a sudden movement from a time of great growth caused by a powerful reinforcing feedback loop to a time of decline caused by a controlling, balancing feedback loop, nonlinearities are at work.

Daniel Aronson, in his article *Overview of Systems Thinking* written in 1996, gives a good example of how systems thinking can work to overcome a problem of nonlinearities.[xxxiv] We are all familiar with the problem of insects eating farmers' crops and the traditional method of solving that problem by spraying pesticides on the crops to kill the insects. For the purpose of sharing his example, Aronson asks us to imagine a perfect pesticide is used that doesn't have any of the potential environmental concerns that pesticides currently do.

A simple diagram would show that as a pesticide is applied, the number of insects goes down. To someone who thinks results are linear, the assumption would be that as more pesticides are applied, more insects will be killed and the crops will be saved. This thesis can prove to be true in the short term.

On the diagram the arrow indicates the direction of the intervention, while "o" means that there is a change happening in an "opposite" direction. When one side goes up; the other side goes down. If we had the letter "s" above the arrow, it would mean that change is happening in the same direction: When one side goes up, the other side will go up too and vice versa.[xxxv]

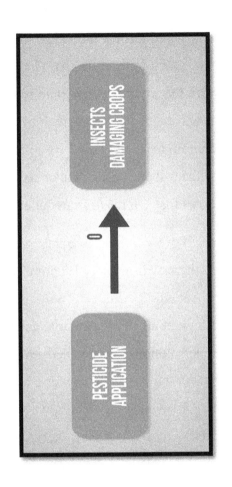

Diagram 8: The relationship between pesticide
application and the insects.[xxxvi]

A systems thinker knows that jumping to conclusions based on an individual event likely won't answer long-term questions. They recognize that they are faced with countless nonlinearities in the world and that often if we rush to embrace a quick solution to a problem, we often do not consider that there are unintended negative consequences that can result from our actions.

Over time, if we continue to apply pesticides to the crops, there will actually be more damage to the crops caused by insects. Why is this? By failing to look at all of the potential consequences of a possible solution, we may inadvertently cause the very result that we were trying to avoid in the long term. As we spray pesticides, we will kill the original insect that was eating the crops. But in doing so, we will also tamper with nature's delicate balance. Once the insects have been killed, other insects in the area will increase in number. This is either due to the first insect no longer being around to act as competition for the other insects or no longer being around to act as a predator keeping the other populations of insects in check from growing too big.

When the other insects in the area increase in number, they will eat more of the crops and it may turn out that even more of the crops will be eaten than would have been if the original insects had just stayed. As a result, our actions caused the problem to get worse on the long run.

Take a look at the diagram. According to the feedback loop, and our short-term expectations, the more pesticide we apply, the less insects we'll have destroying our crops. (Insect A is the original insect we want to get rid of). But the decrease in numbers of insect A inadvertently leads to a boom in the numbers of insect B. (Notice the "o" - opposite direction on the loop.)

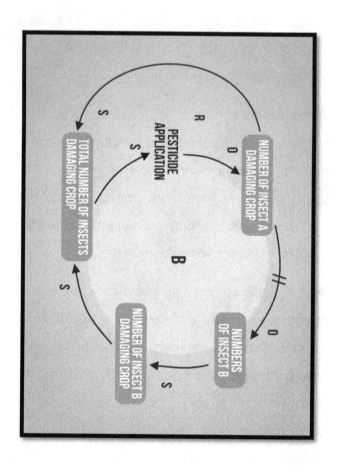

Diagram 9: The balancing (B) and reinforcing (R) feedback loops of the pesticides[xxxvii]

The increase in the number of insect B will lead to more damage to our crops. The more insects there are, the more damage they create. This change happens in the "s" – same direction. While we reached our goal for the short-term and diminished the number of the original insects (insect A), in the long-term, the total number of insects damaging our crops increased. If we stay in this vicious cycle and our response to the increased numbers of insects is the use of even more pesticide, we'll only reinforce the loop we are already in.

Systems thinkers study potential problems by creating a detailed causal loop diagram like Diagram 9 and spending time studying the problem and all potential solutions from every possible angle to be certain they aren't surprised by unintended negative consequences. This allows them to come up with more creative and better solutions. In the case of the pesticides, Aronson suggests that systems thinkers would have been more likely to have come up with a solution like introducing more of the original insect's natural predators into the area. This would have caused their numbers to drop, but not so dramatically that the other insect populations would quickly get out of control, causing the crops to be more protected for the long-term instead of just in the short term.[xxxviii]

Open systems have no boundaries

All systems are connected. There really are no individual separate systems. This is a difficult concept to wrap our heads around. Boundaries are artificially created by people in order to help them to separate and clearly examine one problem at a time. There is no such thing as one correct boundary of a system. The boundaries we decide to draw around systems are based on the questions we are trying to answer and the problems we are trying to solve. The boundaries we draw can lead to problems if we fail to keep in mind that they are of our own making and were artificially created by us.

In a perfect world, we would always study a problem and choose whatever boundary best helped to meet the needs of the system. But we are creatures of habit, and we become comfortable with the boundaries we typically use. To get a more accurate picture, we should create a new boundary for each problem or purpose, have an open mind, and judge every situation on its own merits.

The limits of a system

Just because systems don't have boundaries, it doesn't mean they have no limits. There are limits in place around every system. Our challenge as systems thinkers is to figure out what those limits are and to recognize that growth either diminishes those limits or intensifies them, ultimately changing what limits exist. When one factor in a system is no longer limiting, there will be growth. That growth will impact other factors in a system, either making them more plentiful or sparse until one of those factors becomes the new limiting influence on the system.

Moving our focus from the plentiful factors to the next potentially limiting factor is what understanding and ultimately controlling the growth of a system is all about. As systems grow and develop over time, they interact with each other and impact their own limits. This creates a coevolving dynamic system.

A deeper understanding of the limits currently in place in a system as well as the next potentially limiting factor is not enough to guarantee that the system will continue to grow forever. That simply isn't possible. Just think about population growth, income growth, or even body mass growth. None of these can go on forever. Instead of focusing on trying to achieve never-ending growth it's more useful to establish minimum requirements and acceptable limits the system can live in.

Universities always want to attract more students. They work to create a learning and campus environment that results in happy students because those students will spread the word to others about what a great place it is to go to school there, and more students will enroll. While the university would like to see this growth continue indefinitely, there will ultimately be time limit that prevents them from being able to bring in more students. The biggest issue with on campus student enrollment we've had over the past five years is that classes are taught during certain hours and specific schedules and the ability to find space to teach classes in rooms outside specific spaces has gotten harder and harder – to the point where school starts in a week and I have a class with twenty students enrolled and no assigned meeting space. Going online removes that space issue and even limiting the number students per cohort or per section for QC issues, you can teach multiple sections or run multiple cohorts in a year. Another limit to growth can be the financial aid and scholarships, because at the moment there is only a single federal student load lender now – The US government. All other companies are just processors and those are limited.

We need to accept that there will always be limits to a system's growth. These limits will either be self-imposed or system-imposed. No system can grow forever. If people do not choose to put their own limits in place, the system will automatically do it for them.

Delays

Everything takes time. Whether it is waiting for a cake to bake, waiting for a vacation to begin, waiting for a package to arrive, or waiting to find out how a great mystery novel ends everything takes time – and usually more time than we would like or expect.

Systems, and more importantly system changes, are no exception. Delays are inevitable. Stocks are a delay. Many flows have delays as well. Think about the time a company needs to ship something (processing time), or the delay that the de facto shipping requires. A good wine ages and gets more valuable with time. So does a classic car. Whatever happens to us, we realize it with a perception delay. Some things work on even bigger delays. For example, a change in the incentives to encourage childbirth and rearing in a country wanting to increase its population growth won't show its positive or negative effects for years. People have a perception delay – not everybody will know about the new incentives right away, or be ready to bear and rear children at the time the incentives are announced. There will be a natural, biological delay. Optimally it takes nine months for a child to be born, not considering premature childbirth. It will take months or years to measure longitudinal population growth, analyze the data, conclude that the growth (if there is any) is indeed due to the policy changes and so on. Delays are a fact of life in systems.

When we choose what delays to examine in a system, we should keep our focus on what our current questions and concerns are. If we are interested in analyzing fluctuations or swings that are happening over a span of months, then delays that take minutes or years should not be our immediate focus or concern.

Delays are driving forces behind how fast systems are able to respond to change, whether they are able to achieve their goals, and the speed at which information can be shared within the system. Delays are largely responsible for causing declines, overshoots, and fluctuations within a system.[xxxix]

Bounded Rationality as referred to by Nobel Prize winning economist Herbert Simon

Theodore Roosevelt once said, "Do what you can with what you have where you are." This could be a fair summary of what bounded rationality is. Bounded rationality means that people usually make sensible decisions based on the information that they have. The quality of their decisions is only as good as the information they have. It is impossible to have perfect information, especially about parts of a system that are more distant. Farmers don't know for sure how much rain to expect in a given year, if there be drought, or how the economy will shift. Farmers can only be sure of their sowing and reaping methods and the caretaking of their plants or animals. A famous quote by Robert H. Schuller illustrates this point well. He said, "Anyone can count the seeds in an apple, but only God can count the number of apples in a seed." An apple orchardist can study data from the yields of his trees over time and carefully analyze all aspects of his orchard system, but try as he might, he will never be able to successfully predict the exact number of apples that will grow from each of the seeds (trees) he plants.

Nobel Prize winning economist Herbert Simon explained in his theory of bounded rationality that we are not all-knowing beings. He recognized that there are limits on our decision-making abilities, including our intellectual and reasoning abilities, the quality of the information we have, and the amount of time we have before the decision must be made. When you add to that the fact that humans aren't perfect, you get the need for people to make decisions by what Simon refers to as satisficing: doing the best that we can with what we have.

It is impossible for us to completely predict what others will do in a given situation. This further limits our ability to see every possibility that lies ahead of us and hinders our decision making abilities. We simply have to try to meet our needs as well as we possibly can with our decision, and then move ahead to the next one.

We are human and we make mistakes even in processing and interpreting the information that we have access to. We have to do our best to be open minded and objective as we analyze information and focus less on current events and more on the historical and long term behavior of a system.

If we want to change and improve the quality of the decisions that are being made about a system, simply replacing the current decision maker is not enough. Since our decisions are only as good as the information we have, we need to expand the amount of information we have access to and actually review. This means gathering information from the entire system instead of just certain elements. If the information is not as accessible as the system is, the system needs to undergo some changes that ensure access to the best possible information is being received.

When to intervene in a system?

In the previous section I discussed changing the system to gain better information. I know you may be asking yourself, "how can I change the system? Where should I intervene? How?" I will answer these questions now.

Leverage points

How can we change a system's structure? How do we access more and better information? Ultimately, how can we make the system produce more of the things we want and less of the things we don't? We need to start by finding the system's leverage points. Leverage points are the pieces in a system where making a small change could result in a big difference in behavior. In essence, these are the places in our system where we get the "biggest bang for our buck." We don't have to change much in order to have a big impact. The problem is that people often don't push the change in the right direction. We need to consider a cost-benefit analysis if we move a leverage point in a certain direction. If we don't, we may end up making the problem we are trying to solve worse than it was to begin with.[xl]

Remember the example of the pesticides? Using them was definitely not the best leverage point. Interfering in the balance of nature caused more damage to the crops in the long run. Recall my example with the avalanche. A good leverage point is like hitting the spot on a mountain that would cause the largest avalanche, just as the character Mulan did with the Chinese Army's last cannon in an attempt to use nature to defeat the Huns. (If you have children around the age of twenty-five, thirty, you must know what I'm talking about.)

Changing parameters

A parameter is a characteristic that helps to define and evaluate a system. When we alter the guidelines by which we judge the success of a system or the way that we define the system and its purpose, it can result in major changes to the whole system.

Every time we enter a new election cycle the national debt always becomes a major topic of debate between candidates of both political parties. The national debt is a stock. If the government spends more money or cuts taxes, the nation has a deficit and the national debt increases. If the government cuts spending or raises taxes, the national debt decreases (as long as the increase is greater than the interest payments our country has to make). Our elected officials have to make difficult decisions as to adjust the flows into and out of this system.

These decisions are made all the more difficult because our government officials like to get reelected and the national debt is always a hot button, politically charged issue with both parties blaming each other and arguing over the parameters that impact the size of the debt. The voters are very invested in the monetary flows in this system because they are responsible for paying for the debt. Everyone will tell you that they want the debt to drop, but they do not want to pay more in taxes or have any of the government programs that are important to them cut to reduce spending. This causes great hesitation and anxiety for the government officials because they don't want to upset their constituents so much that they won't reelect them. This approach results is the debt gradually growing no matter who is in office.

Parameters are important but usually only in the short term. Voters feel passionately about them if they are directly impacted by the flows and will make their voices heard on things like wanting subsidies to help pay for rising healthcare or having to pay more in taxes. But changing the parameters in a system rarely result in positive change to how our national economy behaves. They aren't strong enough to bring stability to the system as a whole. Overall, changing parameters in a system is not a quick or impactful way of intervention.

Buffers

A stock that acts to stabilize a system is known as a buffer. Buffers are an added support in place to help a system to stay steady when things go wrong. A buffer is the money in our savings account to help protect us if we have an unexpected expense or run into financial difficulties. We want to have enough batteries and candles in our home in case our power goes out. We want to have enough food in our pantry in case we can't make it to the store. All of these stocks act as buffers.

If we increase the size of the buffer, we get more stability in our system. There is a fine line though. If the size of our buffer becomes too large, we risk having an unyielding and stagnant system resistant to change. For example, if you hoard together a big food supply, you'll need to consume that over time if you don't want it to expire.

Thinking on a larger scale, a power plant, or a water reservoir work as buffers. Big buffers like those respond slowly, repairing and expanding them takes time, and they are not cheap to maintain. Since they are slow to respond and resistant to change, they do not make good leverage points.[xli]

Rules and Incentives

A system's rules define the area it is tasked to work within, its limits, and how much freedom it has. Rules are powerful. When rules change or are restructured, our behavior responds very quickly and changes right along with them. If the speed limit suddenly changes from 75 Mph to 70 Mph you'll automatically adapt to the slower driving speed to avoid speeding tickets. This makes rule changes excellent leverage points. Those who have the power to change the rules hold a great deal of power in their hands.

When things go wrong or right in a system and you are trying to find out why, take a look at the rules that are in place and who has the power to make those rules.

Chapter 6: Examples Of One And Two-Stock Systems

The examples I'm about to discuss are classic systems thinking examples. You can easily find them in other books and online sources if you need more explanation on them.

A One Stock System - Population and the industrial economy

Let's take a look at what happens when a reinforcing loop and a balancing loop are both pulling on the same stock?

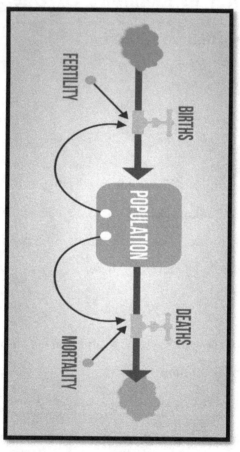

Diagram 10: A stock pulled by a reinforcing (R) and balancing (B) loop.[xlii]

All living populations have a reinforcing loop which allow them to grow through their birth rate and a balancing loop that indicates mortality. If the birth rate was higher than the death rate, the population would grow greatly in a given year as the reinforcing loop would be in control. If the death rate was higher than the birth rate, the balancing loop would be dominant and the population would decrease for that year.

Let's take a population of thirty giraffes. During the course of a year and a half, the giraffes welcomed nine new babies into their herd, while five giraffes died. Since the birth rate was higher than the death rate, the reinforcing loop would be dominant, which would result in the population growing in number.

If during the span of the following year and a half, deforestation occurs, taking away a significant portion of their food and causing eleven giraffes to die while only four newborns arrive, the balancing loop would be in control, and the number of giraffes in the herd would decrease.

If the birth rate and death rate were the same – seven giraffes were born and seven giraffes died during the same period of time – and those rates stayed constant, the giraffe population would level off and enter a state of dynamic equilibrium.

The behavior in the example of the giraffe population demonstrated the shifting dominance of feedback loops. Whatever type of loop is dominant has the most influence on the system and its behavior. When feedback loops operate on the system at the same time, they compete with one another, and the loop that is dominant is the one that determines the behavior. When the reinforcing loop was dominant, the population responded with growth. When the balancing loop is in control, the population declined. If both the reinforcing and balancing loop are the same strength, neither one dominated, and the population leveled off, causing the system to be in dynamic equilibrium.

Whenever you are presented with a prediction, as a systems thinker you will want to dig a little deeper to see if you think it is a solid forecast based on data. The following questions are helpful to consider as you evaluate a prediction:

- **"Are the driving factors likely to behave in the way they suggest?"**

  In our example, the driving factors are the birth and death rates. This is a hard question to answer with certainty because it is asking you to make a guess about the future. The best a systems thinker can do is carefully study the system's behavior over time to explore what would happen if the driving factors behaved in a variety of different ways - in essence studying all possible scenarios. Making predictions in a dynamic system without proper exploration is not a good idea.

173

- **"If the driving factors did behave that way, would the system react this way?"**

  In our example we would ask if the birth and death rates would make the stock (population) respond the way we think it would? This question is a test of the accuracy of the model we use. Regardless of what you believe the driving factors will do, would the system behave as expected?

- **"What is driving the driving factors?"**[xliii]

  In our example, we would examine what is impacting the birth and death rates. This question assesses the boundaries of a system. It examines the driving factors to see if they are acting autonomously or are implanted in the system. There will undoubtedly be multiple forces impacting the driving factors (birth and death rates) coming from both within and outside the system. While the driving factors are themselves feedback loops, they are also influenced by the feedback loops acting upon them.

Let's bring the giraffes into the zoo with many other kinds of animals to demonstrate how economic factors can influence population. Just like the population, the economy is a reinforcing loop-balancing loop system. As a result, it has the same structure and behavior patterns as a population.

A zoo makes money from the people who purchase tickets to visit it. The greater the stock of capital the zoo has in their economy - the number of animals, attractions, vending machines, cafes, and gift shop items to sell - and the efficiency of their production (how well and quickly they can accommodate and please each guest), the more output (goods and services to guests) the zoo will be able to produce in a certain amount of time.

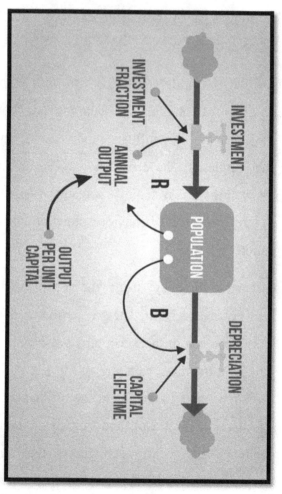

Diagram 11: The behavior of the economy.[xliv]

On Diagram 11, this is illustrated by the capital stock box. One of the inflows a zoo that is operating at a large scale is likely to have is a breeding program. In some cases some inflows may be payments from other zoos for purchases of animals to bread at their zoo. The zoo supplying the animal can have a surplus because of breeding, and the zoo demanding the animal might have a surplus for having a baby animal as a new "asset."

If the zoo produces a lot of output, like being able to offer more shows and attractions, souvenirs, and food for their visitors to buy, they will generate more income, which they can then reinvest back into the zoo. By reinvesting that capital, they will be able to purchase, feed, and care for more animals, build and make improvements to their attractions and facilities, hire more employees, and purchase more food and souvenirs to sell, etc. This will help them make even more income. This is a reinforcing loop that works just like the birth rate reinforcing loop in our previous example. The more output the zoo is able to reinvest, the faster it will be able to grow its stock of physical capital. We can see this process on Diagram 11 where though there is a dominant reinforcing feedback loop (R) the output is reinvested, ensuring a stable growth to the zoo.

Unfortunately, not only growth can happen to a business. The animals, if they became injured, sick, or even die, that decline in the stock would act like a death rate in the population example. Every attraction and facility depreciates and suffers from wear and tear over time or becomes less popular with guests, which may mean they can no longer be used by the zoo. The longer the zoo is able to take good care of everything and keep using their physical capital, the less capital they will need to accept losing or replace each year. On Diagram 11, we can see this process through the balancing feedback loop (B) that affects the depreciation.

If the zoo's reinforcing loop is dominant, it will be able to reinvest more money back into the system and upgrade or purchase new capital to assure further growth. If the zoo's balancing loop is in control, the zoo will have to retire and replace more capital instead of increasing their stock. This will result in the growth slowing down or dying off. If neither the reinforcing nor the balancing loop is dominant, the system will level off and stay constant in a state of dynamic equilibrium. Whether this system grows, dies off, or remains constant depends on:

- how much output the system invests
- how efficiently can the capital create a unit of output
- the lifespan of the capital

There are two ways to make a stock grow: increase its inflow or reduce its outflow. In our zoo example, the stock could grow if more animals, food, souvenirs, attractions, and facilities were purchased (increasing the inflow) or by taking such good care of the existing capital (animals, facilities, attractions, employees, etc.) that it would not have to be retired or replaced for as long as possible, thus reducing its outflow.

A key understanding of systems theory, just as important as recognizing that systems largely cause their own behavior, is that systems with the same structures will exhibit the same dynamic behaviors even when at first glance you think that the systems couldn't be more different. Both the economy and a population are able to reproduce themselves – money makes money and giraffes make giraffes. Giraffes age and die. Also money uses it's value over time due to inflation, the actual paper the money is made of ages, and becomes unusable thus the physical paper money needs to be changed.

In the large-scale view of economic development, analyzing population and economic growth together is one of the most important research topics investigated. The answer these researchers are seeking is how to make the reinforcing loop of capital creation work faster than the reinforcing loop of population growth. In other words, if the population grows faster than wealth, people will get poorer and poorer. If a country's or the general common wealth grows faster than the population, people will generally live better. This, of course, is an incomplete model that assumes that wealth distribution is equal. In reality, wealth distribution is far from being equal. In real life rich get richer and poor get poorer. How and why? I will talk about it in the following chapters.

A Renewable Stock Constrained by a Nonrenewable Stock [xlv]

In our previous examples we talked about the population and the economy. These were both examples of one-stock systems. Now I will present a system that has two stocks, a renewable and a nonrenewable.

Everything tangible in this world exchanges things with the environment surrounding it. A school needs students, teachers, water, and electricity among other things to function. An animal needs food, water, shelter, and a habitat to survive. Because of biological, physical, and chemical needs – energy, waste disposal, space - growing systems, influenced by a reinforcing loop, will ultimately encounter a limitation, which will take the form of a balancing loop. Even when a balancing loop isn't dominant, we know of its existence because it's impossible for any real physical system to keep growing forever. Systems theory calls this phenomenon the "limits-to-growth" archetype.

Resources provide the inflow to the stock and are either renewable or nonrenewable. Renewable resources are resources like oxygen, water, wind, and solar energy which can be used over and over and are replaced by nature before they are completely consumed. Nonrenewable resources are resources like coal, oil, and natural gas that take so long to be replaced by nature that they can't be replaced as fast as they are being used. It's important to make the same distinction with pollutants, which can also be renewable or nonrenewable. A pollutant is renewable if the environment has a fixed ability to remove it. A pollutant is nonrenewable if the environment has no ability to absorb the pollutant or make it less harmful.[xlvi]

Let's see the behavior of an oil company on Diagram 12.

The balancing loop (B1) drives depreciation and may represent the machinery of the company such as the extracting and refining equipment. If we estimate an average lifetime of about twenty-five years for these machines, this means the oil company will lose 1/25 of its capital stock each year.

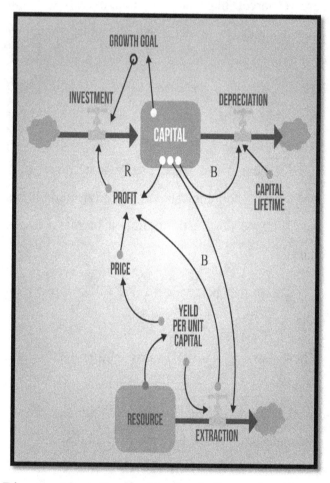

Diagram 12: A Renewable Stock Constrained by a Nonrenewable Stock.[xlvii]

In other words, four percent of this company's commission will be gone on it's very first day of operation.

This system grows when a reinforcing loop (R) is dominant. With reinvesting it's profit (income – cost), the oil company will be able to extract more oil, which in turn will lead to the company making greater profit that can then be reinvested in order to keep the growth going at a more rapid rate.

Since oil is a nonrenewable resource, the stock fostering the extraction doesn't have an input. As you can see in diagram 12, the oil box only has an output. When an oil company removes the oil, the oilfield becomes depleted over time. With each barrel of oil they mine, the job of the oil company becomes more difficult. When they drill for each additional barrel, they will have to dig deeper because the stock has decreased and there is less natural pressure to force more oil closer to the surface. The company has to spend more and more money effectively mining oil.

This acts as another balancing loop on the system that limits the growth of its capital (B2). When the oil company has a lot of capital, it can extract a lot of oil. As it extracts more oil, there are fewer resources available. When there are fewer resources, they will get less yield from each unit of capital they spend. This means that they will make less profit (for the purpose of this example we are assuming that the price they can charge for a barrel of oil remains constant) and thus have less money to reinvest, which means their capital will grow at a slower pace.

When the oil company first starts to drill in an oilfield, there is enough of a supply that, if the difficulty and cost of extraction didn't increase, the extractable oil it would last for 100 years. But the actual depletion time depends on many factor like consumption over time, the speed and amount of extraction per year, the number of drills, etc. The extraction will reach its optimal limit much quicker than expected also due to the aforementioned increasing extraction costs causing the extraction to slow, having less yield per unit of capital. The company will reach a point where the costs will be so significant that the income they earn from extracting the oil isn't enough to keep the level of investment ahead of the level of depreciation. The capital stock decreases and the drilling shuts down, abandoning the oil left in the ground because the cost of extracting it wouldn't be worth the costs. The same happens with any system whose growth depends on nonrenewable resources. The faster the system grows in such cases, the faster it will fall. The faster the extraction rate, the faster the resource(s) will get depleted. The ultimate decision a company has to make in the case of a nonrenewable resource is to get rich quickly or stay in business longer.

This example was a simplification of the real world, of course. We assumed that oil prices stay constant, that no new oil fields will be discovered, and no natural event or force majeure affects the extraction process. We also didn't consider the negative natural consequences a fast extraction can cause. Let's imagine what would happen if oil prices increased. In this case, the company would have more profit to invest in either faster extraction and the critical point of when the oil extraction would not be worth the cost would come later. Conversely, if oil price dropped, the company would be out of business faster or find new, untapped oilfields.

As we discussed earlier, there are two ways to increase stock: by increasing the inflow (as the higher price charged brought in more profits to the company that they reinvested) or by reducing the outflow. In the case of our oil company, reducing the outflow of stock might be caused by technological advances which make it cheaper and easier to extract the remaining oil from the field, thus causing the company's operating costs to drop.

As long as systems depend on nonrenewable resources to grow their stock, the dynamics of depletion will be in play. An oil company knows that the supply of oil in a field will ultimately become depleted and too costly to extract, causing them to abandon the field. They are always on the lookout for the next place they can drill. The larger the stock of oil they have to begin with, the longer the reinforcing loop will be dominant over the balancing loop. The higher the capital stock and the cost of extracting it the earlier, faster, and further the fall will be after the system hits its production peak. As they say, the bigger they are, the harder they fall.

Big oil companies know the risks of quick depletion and increased costs so they start to scout a new location for oil extraction before the old one runs out and start doing business at the new place, too. Think of Halliburton, a huge oil company in Texas. Oil and gas is one of their biggest industries there. Halliburton doesn't drill exclusively in Texas. It also drills in the Middle East. When Halliburton wanted to go into Iraq after its second war with the US to help "rebuild" it was granted a lot of government contracts to do that. (But then Dick Cheney, the Vice President at the time, was also the former CEO of Halliburton.) The point being, big firms look for new opportunities before the renewable resource runs out. [xlviii]

There are systems where a renewable stock is constrained by generation. A good example could the lumber industry. In the case of renewable sources, the extraction flow can be limited. A renewable source can support extraction indefinitely, especially since a wood exporting company is likely getting lumber form multiple sources but only with a flow rate that matches the regeneration rate. If the extracting company doesn't respect the thin balance of flow and regeneration and overexploits the stock, the renewable source might become nonrenewable (extinct in other words).

Chapter 7: Systems Archetypes

System archetypes are commonly repeating variations of reinforcing and balancing feedback. Each archetype has a typical pattern of behavior over time, structure, and effective interventions.

These archetypes help us to understand and quickly diagram the behavior of a system. The more you practice system analysis, the easier will you notice and apply the structure when hearing an archetypical systems story.[xlix]

Some systems can cause troublesome behavior through their structure. This trouble can take many forms. Some of the behaviors these archetypes create include addiction, low performance, and escalation. It isn't enough to just recognize the troublemaking structures and understand the problems they cause. They need to be changed.

People often make the mistake of trying to blame other people or events for the destruction these archetypes cause. In reality, the fault lies within the structure of the system. So what can be done? We can escape these so called system traps by being aware of their existence and use that knowledge to avoid getting caught in them. We can change the structure by revisiting our goals and developing new ones. We can work with the feedback loops to strengthen, weaken, or alter them or even add new ones to the system.

The system archetypes rapidly build systemic awareness and provide a simple and engaging way to communicate about systems to others who may have no Systems Thinking background. They are easy to understand. Working with classic stories helps people shift their thinking to a more systemic perspective. The classic stories are also an easy means of transferring learning about systemic issues from one situation to another.

If you successfully master the systems archetypes, you'll be familiar with the storylines and regular patterns of behavior over time. You'll detect them in real-world events and map their structure with ease. Also, by Going Deeper™ you'll be able to improve and enrich the structure of the specific system you'll be analyzing, adding implications for leveraged interventions.

The nine most common systems archetypes are the following:

- Shifting the Burden
- Fixes that Backfire
- Growth and Underinvestment
- Tragedy of the Commons
- Limits to Success
- Accidental Adversaries
- Escalation
- Drifting Goals

- Success to the Successful

I will review four of the nine archetypes mentioned above: the tragedy of the commons, the success to the successful, escalation, and shifting the burden. The other archetypes can easily be located online if you want to deepen your knowledge about them.

Tragedy of the Commons

The tragedy of the commons is a trap that appears when there is escalation in a shared, erodible environment.

In the United States there is no limit on who is able to own a car or how many cars a person is allowed to own. In fact, in 2016, there were 268.8 million vehicles registered in the United States with about 95% of households owning at least one car.

This was not always the case. Until the late 1940s, at least 40% of households didn't own a car as they lived mostly in cities and depended on public transportation to get from place to place. Since the 1960s, the number of cars owned in the United States has continued to grow.

Why is this? As people began to move out of cities and into suburbs, they found they could purchase a house for less money and purchase a car to commute to work. The highway system continued to grow and be improved, so people found it more convenient to be able to drive themselves around. Not to mentions those suburbs that didn't have well operating public transportation.

Car owners have the commonly shared environment of our roads and highways and they share the need for oil and gas, bot nonrenewable resources. In addition to the conveniences we have already mentioned, car owners have the freedom to drive themselves anywhere they want anytime they want without being tied to a public transportation schedule. For many, owning a car is even a status symbol.

The downside to this increased growth in car ownership is that there is a finite amount of oil and products made from available to us on Earth as it is a nonrenewable resource that we are consuming it faster than it can be replaced. The oil is consumed even faster because there are so many cars on the road. Another problem is that more cars on the road means more pollution enters the air, which can be a contributing factor to climate change and health problems.

Additionally, as more cars travel on our roadways, there is increased wear and tear on them. This can render some roads and bridges unsafe to travel on, and can result in costly repairs of which all taxpayers share the financial burden. Not to mention the costs of insurance of drivers who don't carry it despite it being a legal requirement. The increase of cars also means an increase in accidents, which tax emergency rooms. We can see the ripple effect here.

In this example, car ownership has increased in number consistently since the 1960s. Car ownership was encouraged to help financially support the auto industry and touted as a symbol of status. For the city banker it was a sensible decision to own car because it provided him the freedom to be able to travel as he wish without being limited by a public transportation schedule. The only problem was that every other car buyer came to the same conclusion, and soon the highways and roads were invaded with hour-long traffic jams. Some families end up owning as many as one car per family member. This can mean four or five cars per family. One car usually has five seats that could easily serve the family of five, but due to increased desire for comfort, a high percentage of cars driven on the streets has only one passenger. When a couple work in totally different areas and both live far from their workplace, having two cars is reasonable.

The infrastructure of roadways and the highway system continued to grow and improve to serve the growing demand. Car owners understood that if improvements and repairs to roads were necessary, the cost would be shared by everyone so that wasn't a big deterrent to purchasing a car.

Car owners share the common environment of the roads, bridges, and highway system as well as the nonrenewable resource of oil. This common environment can be destroyed by consumption over time because there will be increased deterioration on the roads due to the escalation in the number of cars being driven on it. The roads and bridges may be rendered unsafe for travel or require costly repairs. Also, the amount of oil is being consumed faster than it can be replaced so eventually the resource will be depleted. Finally, the pollution created by the cars is detrimental to the environment and could be a contributing factor to climate change and quality of health. All of these negative consequences are examples of the troublesome behaviors exhibited by this system.

How to fix the tragedy of the commons?

Educate and warn people about the consequences of uncontrolled use of the commons. Make your statements appeal to their morality. Make people aware of the collective costs of their individual actions. Use persuasive language or illustrations to influence peoples' sense of austerity. If sensibility is not motivating enough, use threatening future predictions, mention the possibility of social disapproval. Focus on the greater common good.

Privatization can be a helpful and just system to save the commons. This way people will need to own their actions, and fix whatever they personally damaged. If someone can't control him or herself in overexploiting his or her private resources, they will cause damage mostly to themselves.

Regulation is a powerful tool to save the commons. We saw earlier how powerful and quick leverage point changes to the rules can be. Bans or restrictions on some behaviors, quotas, taxes, or incentives can all work. Deterring regulations by charging fines or requiring licensing can also be an effective way to stop people from overexploiting the commons.[1]

Success to the successful

Those who are financially well off often use the wealth and privilege they have to get special or additional knowledge, which in turn helps them generate more of the money, privilege, and closed-group information for themselves. Competitive exclusion is a system trap.

Think about what happens when someone wins a competition? They get a reward. This reward — monetary, equipment, granted access, promotions, sponsors — gives the winner the ability to compete even better or easier next time. This forms a reinforcing feedback loop, which increases the likelihood that the winners will keep winning. Consequently, the losers will lose again.

How does Monopoly™, the board game, evolve? Each player begins the game on a level playing field, but as soon as a player begins to accumulate properties on the game board, the game dynamic changes. When a player has control of a property, they can start to build houses and hotels and charge the other players rent when they land on their properties. That player can then take the money they receive from the other players and use it to buy more properties and put more hotels on the game board. This makes it next to impossible for the other players to catch up, and greatly increases the likelihood that the hotel-owning player will win the game.

Sure enough, multiplayers can and build their own hotels. One of the keys can be owning a block of properties in full line or a corner so that all players are going to have to hit your properties every rotation around the board. There's no limit to who can buy what property or what houses and hotels outside the rules. Monopoly™ is a game of strategy of how you come to own the most strategic properties and then make the most money from them to bankrupt the other players... The player who buys hotels first can only retain exclusive power if he plays smart enough to buy further hotels on strategic locations. The first buyer has the advantage to control the game only if he keeps growing strategically to other players disadvantaged. (A hotel on Mediterranean Ave is a waste of money if you ask me.)

Now consider college football teams in the United States. There is a playoff system which determines the national champion each year. The final four teams play against each other in the playoff. For the past few years, it seems that the same two-three teams monopolized playing in the playoff. As college football teams begin winning games, they are given a reward of more access to television time. This increased time on television allows them to increase their fan bases, bring more revenue into their programs, and attract more recruits to their teams. As the teams are more visible, they can generate more money through ticket sales and booster donations. This allows them to hire the best coaches and build the best facilities at their schools.

These events in turn entice the best players to join their football programs, which increases the likelihood that they will continue to win and be successful. The reinforcing feedback loop has now become created and entrenched in their systems.

There are exceptions to this rule, too. Clemson Tigers of South Carolina's Clemson University, which did not even win a conference championship under its previous coach Tommy Bowden, went to winning a national championship under Dabo Swinney in 2017. Swinney had been a coordinator at Clemson before took on the head coach position mid-season in 2008. His greatest asset as a coach is that he is an amazing recruiter.[li] Alabama has been in the championships since Nick Saban took over in 2007, and the success to the successful case applies to their case 100 percent but a lot depends on the coach and his coaching, and also what conference the school plays in. SEC, ACC, Big Ten, Big 12, PAC 12, these all have way more clout. And because the teams aren't playing division II ball in a region where no one cares about college ball. Traditionally these regions are home to the oldest and most prestigious colleges and so that history brings a lot of rivalry and tradition - and football is one of those rivalries and traditions... Just like sculling at the Ivies and Pacific NW.

We also see the success to the successful archetype at play in nature. The competitive exclusion principle tells us that it is impossible to have two different species living in exactly the same ecological niche, competing with one another for exactly the same food and resources. When two species are different, one of the species will either be able to reproduce faster or be more effective at using resources than the other species. This will serve to give that species an advantage over the other one as it will begin to increase its population and continue to be dominant over the other species. The dominant species does not need to fight the other species. By using up all of the available resources, it means there are none left for the weaker competitor. This will force that species to either move away, adapt by using different resources, or become extinct.

Diagram 13 has two reinforcing loops linked by the "allocation of resources" stock. The reinforcing loop on the left (R1) presents the rich get richer scenario.

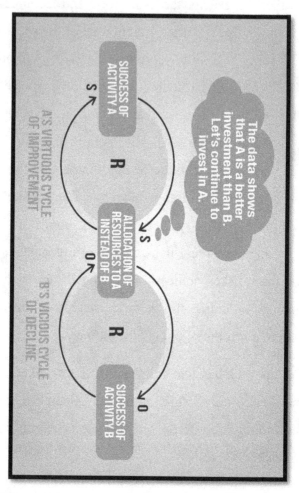

Diagram 13: Success to the successful.[lii]

The more resources A allocates, the more he will have to invest, which will further enrich his stock. The other reinforcing feedback is a vicious cycle of diminishing success for B, the less wealthy.

The "poor get poorer" just the way diagram 13 illustrates. Kids coming from families with less resources usually have access to worse education than their wealthy peers, and thus they end up having lower skilled jobs and lower income levels. Their poverty is reinforced at each stage of life. People who do not have a lot of money are either unable to qualify for loans, or must pay a disproportionately high interest rate compared to the wealthy — whose money banks are using to lend. This keeps the less wealthy from being able to make investments and improve their futures in the same way the wealthy can. People with low incomes are often unable to own their own homes.[liii] They pay rent to those who can afford to own property. Tenants supply landlords, whether with a stable income source or with enough funds to buy a new property for more people to rent. Real life Monopoly™, folks.

Those who earn the least, tend to pay a greater percentage of their income to taxes and healthcare. Wealthy individuals have access to attorneys who can help them find loopholes in the tax code and avoid paying a comparable amount of their income in taxes. This being said, I find it important to mention that the wealthiest one percent of Americans pay the vast majority of American taxes. They pay a smaller percentage, but that percentage still quantifies to a lot of money. The percentage less wealthy people pay is going to be a larger percentage of their income, but it's a lot less money, practically speaking. What is more, five percent of one billion dollars or fifty percent of fifty thousand? Less wealthy people get tax credits and tax cuts too. The problem doesn't reside only in the taxing system, but the very small income some people have. I would gladly pay more taxes if I made double than I do.

Often, people are able to receive discounts when they purchase items in bulk. Research has found that the "bulk-rule" is generally inaccurate in the case of perishable goods. The average family of four isn't going to use large bulk sizes of items before they spoil. Who is using ten pounds of ranch dressing before it spoils? The only person I can imagine is pouring it in a glass and drinking it. A lot of bulk purchases go to waste and thus the person would just be wasting his money while trying to save.[liv]

This doesn't mean purchases at bulk stores don't save money on non-perishable items. Purchases on diapers, meats, vitamins are all much cheaper, but these usually are just slight larger package sizing. Because the less wealthy are still unable to afford these large purchases, they often have to pay higher per piece prices. Other possible scenarios may have a harder toll on the less wealthy that reinforces the vicious loop in which they are stuck. These scenarios might be such as being exposed to more pollution and higher stress levels because they are more like likely to rely on public transportation where the breathe in the exhaust of a bus while waiting for their bus line. And the physician cope with the physical and mental diseases of low-paying jobs that don't provide healthcare and take a toll on a person's body.

The mental model of the "success to the successful," presents only a fraction of reality. Like every other model, it is simplified. It doesn't take into consideration the position of the middle-class, for instance. It's not deemed to reflect reality as it is, it's rather a simplification of reality to illustrate with a visual, but extreme example how the archetype works.

What's the solution for this scenario?

When allocating their resources, people don't always understand the driving factors of the allocations or the impact of their decisions. Sometimes even the appearance of success is enough to get the resources for actual success. Let me illustrate this with a joke.

"A young man wants to marry Bill Gates' daughter. He goes to Bill Gates and asks for his daughter's hand in marriage. The billionaire suspiciously asks the young man:

- Who are you? I will only marry my daughter to the CEO of The Bank of America.
- No problem, says the young man and leaves.

He goes to the Bank of America, applying for the CEO position. When he gets interviewed, the interviewers ask who he is:

- I'm the future son-in-law of Bill Gates, he replies…"

This joke shows how potential can be confused with or sold as achievement and how the appearance of success is critical to secure future, actual success. When we decide to support one party that can involuntarily cause the decline of other parties, it takes clarity about what actually drives one entity's success or the other's to avoid an unwanted outcome.

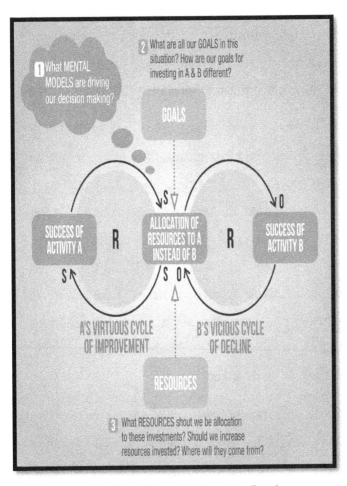

Diagram 14: Possible solutions to fix the success to the successful archetype.[lv]

In solving the conundrum of how can we help a more equal resource allocation we need to develop awareness of how investment decisions influence the outcomes and the investment decisions of the future.

Make well-rounded, clear goals and commit to wish success for all parties. The potential of each activity should be measured separately. After carefully analyzing this data, create resource allocation policies based on needs and the success of each activity on its own merits. Take a look on whether one's success causes the others' failure or not. Also consider if one's failure influences the successful party in any way?

Create mental models to answer questions like "how might we have created a defensive routine where we assume one party is inherently better than the other, but have only made it so by our own actions?"[lvi]

To get rid of competition or useless comparisons, break or depower the resource link.

Escalation

If you have ever witnessed two siblings fighting with one another, with each new poke, push, or insult getting stronger and worse than the last, you have seen escalation firsthand. Escalation is guided by a reinforcing loop in which the actors involved are in competition with each another and the driving factor behind their behavior and decision making is trying to outdo one another. If the competition brings improvements into the world, we can consider escalation a good thing.

Escalation, however, can also be extremely dangerous. When countries around the world race to build up their nuclear weapons faster than the others, there can be very serious and life threatening consequences. The Cold War is an excellent example of negative escalation. Another example is when two people are drag racing and they continue to push harder and harder, trying to beat their competition, prompting them to make more and more careless choices until someone gets hurt.

One very common display of escalation in our country, and around the world today, involves the use of cyberbullying. The internet and social media can be great tools to help make us all interconnected and able to share and access information like never before. However, some people feel emboldened by the "anonymity" that these virtual platforms afford and think they can make any cruel and negative comment about others without consequence. It is rare to read where someone has even done something as seemingly innocent as shared a recipe or written a review of a product without seeing negative comments not designed to offer helpful constructive criticism, but are instead intended to be quite hurtful and personal. It usually isn't long before you see two or more people begin to argue back and forth, hurling more and more hateful insults at one another. Rapidly, those comments become more about hurting the other person and getting the bigger response from others who are reading the comments and egging them on, encouraging the negative words to continue than whatever they were commenting on in the first place. In some cases cyberbullying has such horrifying and dangerous unintended consequences as teenage suicide. Resulting from cruel and hateful comments some people feel so attacked by their peers and strangers on the internet that they decide to take their own life because they think they will never be able to escape from the damage that has been done to their reputation. A child whose brain isn't cognitively formed doesn't have the capacity to understand the permanence of suicide and that life gets better.

Not all systems that exhibit escalation are so dire and dangerous. In fact, there are several instances when escalation has ended up being beneficial to our society and the world when the goals were nobler and led to a race to find important new scientific discoveries, create helpful new inventions and improvements in technology, develop new medicines, or find the cures for diseases.

But there is a reason that escalation is a behavior archetype. Even in the best situations, escalation can still cause troublesome behavior. No matter the goal or purpose, escalation can grow swiftly, often faster than anyone anticipates, and it can ultimately result in one or both of the competing parties, breaking down completely if nothing is done to break the loop.

How to get out of an escalating situation?

The best is to avoid engaging in it in the first place. But if you find yourself, or a system, already in an escalating situation, you can try the following things:

Become fully aware of the dynamics of this system, its activity level, and the costs.

- Put your mental models about this escalation under a microscope. What do you think about the escalation? Is it a zero-sum game or would the parties be willing to come to an agreement?

- What do you predict will happen if you tried to break the loop and escape this system trap by unilaterally withdrawing from the competition?

- How could each involved party achieve their goals? What are your goals? Do you have any personal goals or is all that matters to you is outdoing your competitor? If so, can you refocus your objectives?

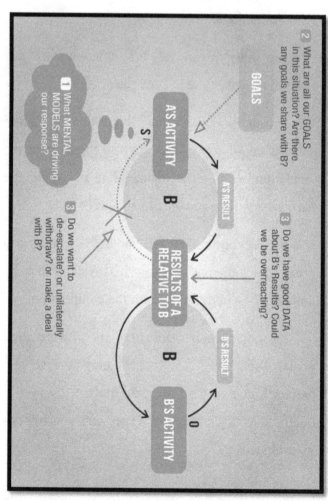

Diagram 15: Possible solutions to escalation.[lvii]

- Are you sure you have an accurate assessment of your competition? Can you get more or more accurate information?

- Try to negotiate different system rules using balancing loops to control the reinforcing loop the escalation operates in.

Shifting the Burden – Addiction

It's hard to turn a blind eye on the addictions that exist in our society today: drugs, alcohol, nicotine, food, shopping, gambling, etc. We are familiar with the unfortunate existence of them.

But there are, however, other kinds of addictions present in many systems that you have probably never thought of as addictions before. An addiction is a reliance or dependence on something such as a country receiving government subsidies for financial loans and support. Many areas of our economy receive government subsidies like the energy, agricultural, and transportation sectors, just to name a few. Farmers can have non-negotiable business standards in the form of a reliance on pesticides and fertilizers to help protect their crops from being eaten by insects and to produce greater yields.

Addictions can involve a physical good like being dependent on painkillers or a feeling like making someone feel a sense of confidence and greater self-worth. No matter the form that an addiction takes, the structure of the system looks the same. It has a stock with inflows and outflows. The stock can be something tangible, like crops, or intangible, like our self-esteem. The decision maker of the stock adjusts the balancing feedback loop by changing either the inflow or the outflow.[lviii]

When we intervene by granting a subsidy or providing a good to solve a problem within a system, the short-term results can be very positive and make us think that a solution has been achieved. In reality, by shifting the burden to the intervention, we won't achieve lasting positive results. The subsidy won't last forever or our bodies and diseases will build up a tolerance to a medicine that eventually becomes ineffective. It is then that we will fall back into the same old problems. This is because we put a Band-Aid™ on a problem for a quick fix without digging deeper to really uncover its root cause and putting in the hard work to solve it for the long-term.

It is often then that the interventionist will try to pour in more of the "solution" that "worked" before, thinking that it will work again. This increases the addiction and dependence on the intervention and weakens the system further, making it unable to make its own corrections to solve the problem.

In other words, the problem recurs despite our repeated efforts to fix it. Over time, the problem will require more of the "fix" to stay under control, often given by someone or something outside of the affected system. The real cause of the problem is either hard to identify or seems impossible to address.

If addiction has taken over, there will be a period of painful withdrawal, whether physical or emotional, in order to finally break free from the cycle. It is best to not fall into the detrimental trap of addiction in the first place.

How can we avoid the trap?

When it becomes clear that a system requires some outside intervention, step in to help temporarily. Make sure that the intervention is not going to become a crutch that the system will become dependent upon, but rather that it will act to strengthen the system so that it can function on its own and solve its own problems in the future. As soon as the system is strong enough, the intervening force should be removed.

It is similar to a strategy used by the military when they go into a country needing protection and assistance. The military trains the troops of the country in need and stays long enough to work alongside them and stabilize the situation. Then they slowly begin to remove themselves until that country is able to rely on their own troops to solve their own problems.

The already-mentioned Chinese proverb states "Give a man a fish and you feed him for a day. Teach a man to fish and you feed him for a lifetime." It is a good thing to remember in dealing with the "shifting the burden" archetype. If you intervene by giving it a quick fix, it won't be a lasting solution, and the system will have the same problems as before and remain dependent upon you and the intervention. But if you strengthen the system and help it to improve so that it is capable of solving its own problems, the system will be able to carry on long after the intervention has been removed and find real and lasting solutions.

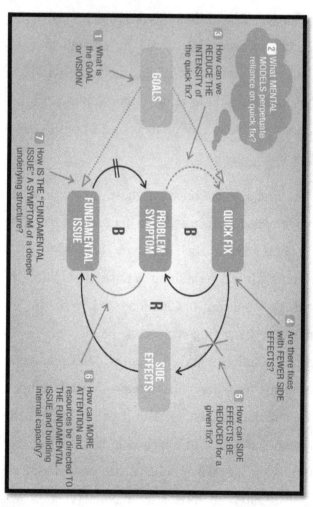

Diagram 16: Possible solutions to the shifting the burden archetype[lix]

228

What is the goal of the system? Try to clarify the real goal. Allocate and highlight if there is a tendency to focus on seemingly urgent local issues and address the mental models that seem to strengthen dependence on the quick fix.

Considering the goals, weaken or break the connection between the symptom and the quick fix. Do this by providing as little of the fix as possible. If the symptoms need to be addressed, try to find a substitute fix with less side effects or with long-term benefits.

It the implementation of negative short-term solutions is unavoidable, try to apply the fix so that you'll limit the consequences as much as you can.

Try to balance the short-term and long-term solutions. Most often this means empowering the link between the real problem and the symptom.

Look for ways to balance short and long-term approaches. In most cases this means strengthening the link between the symptom and the fundamental issue. Be aware and ask yourself if the seemingly "fundamental issue" is just another symptom? If you confirm this suspicion, dig deeper to identify the real cause of the addiction and new ways to address it.[lx]

Chapter 8: Systems Thinking in Social Matters

When we recognize that there is a gap between where we currently are and where we want to be, we begin to become motivated to make a change and do something about it. In a system, when we reach that conclusion collectively and begin to create a shared vision, mission, and set of core values together on which we can all agree, we are taking the first steps toward being able to create meaningful and lasting change.

But that alone is not enough. We also need to dig deeper into the system to make sure everyone is on the same page in evaluating not only where the system currently is, but also *why* it is there. That is when people truly start feeling invested and engaged in wanting to be a part of the solution.

231

They begin to go beyond taking responsibility just for their individual task within the system to recognizing that they also play an important role in how the entire system performs. They have more of a stake in the game and will take more ownership over the results.

Often when we try to solve a problem, we end up causing more of the very behavior that we are hoping to avoid in the first place. That is because the problems often lie in the system's structure. As David Peter Stroh, the author of the book *Systems Thinking for Social Change*[lxi] says, "organizations and social systems have a life of their own." We might wish to push the system in a positive direction and the system would still operate the same way as always as if no intervention had happened. Why? Most probably because it didn't get the right push.

If we don't do our homework and dig deeper into the system to get to the real root of the problem instead of being satisfied with a quick fix, we are wasting our time and energy because we won't be able to solve these problems in the long run.

Good Intentions

Business consultant James C. Collins once said, "Bad decisions made with good intentions, are still bad decisions." Good intentions are simply not enough. We all mean well, but sometimes in a rush to find a solution we actually make things worse. It is important to own it when a solution isn't working and begin putting in the work to effect meaningful change.

Here are just a few examples of solutions gone wrong despite everyone's best intentions:

- Countries with the most restrictive abortion laws have the highest rates of abortion.
  A 2018 study conducted by the Guttmacher Institute found that the

abortion rates worldwide have fallen during the last twenty-five years even though more countries have legalized abortion and made the procedures easier to get. Making abortion illegal is intended to decrease the number of women getting abortions, but it seems to have the opposite effect.[lxii]

- States where the death penalty is legal have consistently higher murder rates than states where the death penalty is illegal. The Death Penalty Information Center has gathered statistics on murder rates in all 50 states from 1990-2016 using U.S. Census data and published reports on crime from the F.B.I. Every year during that time span the murder rates were lower in states that do not have the death penalty than in states that do. Obviously, instituting the death penalty as a possible punishment was intended to deter people from committing heinous crimes like murder, but according to the statistics, this is another solution gone wrong.[lxiii]

There are many more examples of failed solutions that were created with the best of intentions. Everything from the increased availability of job training programs not resulting in lower unemployment to the war on drugs contributing to additional problems it never intended even as addiction and drug abuse continue to be a major problem in modern society. There is no shortage of well-intentioned solutions that have failed to bring the results people expected or were promised.

When a judge decides to incarcerate a parent who commits a crime, he or she does it with good intentions such as keeping a criminal off the streets, and because it's required by the law. (I wish to stress here that I'm talking about minor law infringements. I would never suggest a serial killer, or child abuser to be spared just because he or she has a child.) For whatever reason the parent is incarcerated, the child will suffer greatly by not having a complete, healthy family. He or she might end up in foster care. Growing up under such circumstances, being in multiple homes where the child may have felt unwanted, was socioeconomically at risk, and lack strong values and identity provided by a family unit, may lead this child to a criminal path later in life as a consequence of the parent's original criminal activity. The judge shifted the burden, but created ripple effect. It is essential to recognize one's contribution to an unwanted consequence. When one recognizes and accepts his or her responsibility in the creation of a problem, only then can better solutions be found.

Good intentions are simply not enough. When it comes to dealing with complex, chronic social issues, applying conventional linear thinking and quick fixes will not be enough to generate the desired real and lasting solutions.

When people are unified around the common ground of a shared vision, mission, purpose, and set of goals because they have done the work of taking a hard, honest, and objective look at where the system currently is, better solutions could be found. This unification, however, is more difficult than it sounds. It's not like we are going to agree when we identify a social issue, sit down and sing *Kumbaya, My Lord* and solve our nation's deepest social crises by having some conferences and movement. It's going to take a lot of work to bring the majority of people to the table to even have a conversation to start making the changes. Just to bring them to the conversation table before any other hard work is done takes a lot of time. And there will always be outliers that won't join in the conversation and we can't let ourselves be stopped by that.

The individual responsibility in contributing to find a common solution which takes everybody's needs into consideration is invaluable. People who are focused and committed to achieving a goal, put this goal ahead of their own personal interests because they feel empowered to make meaningful and lasting change. It allows everyone to be able to streamline their communication and align their efforts as they keep their eyes on the prize, knowing what needs to be done.

It is important to remember that when you fix a system by restructuring it, there is usually a period of time when things get worse before they get better. If you are able to put in some short-term goals that are aligned with the overarching long-term ones, you might be able to build in some small successes along the way to help everyone through the growing pains and maintain hope that things are moving in the right direction. This will help to keep up their motivation and buy in as they continue to working toward achieving the long-term goal.[lxiv]

The difference between conventional and systems thinking

Conventional thinking has been our more traditional way of addressing problems, and it couldn't be more different from a systems thinking approach. Conventional thinking is looking at things through the lens of cause and effect. It tends to view things as a step-by-step, sequential process with a definite beginning and ending. Conventional thinkers believe that it is easy to find the cause of a problem because it's obvious. They tend to place the blame on people and situations outside of their organization or system when things go wrong. Since they believe others and outside forces are the things that need to change, they rarely reflect inwardly on what role they may have played in causing or contributing to the problem.

Conventional thinkers are focused on the parts of a system rather than the entire system. They believe that improving the parts is the way to improve the whole system. A plan leading to short term success will automatically translate to long-term success in conventional thinkers' understanding. They often work on many strategies independently at the same time, which addresses the symptoms instead of the root of the problem.

In contrast, systems thinking is a paradigm shift that focuses on asking better questions before jumping to conclusions. Systems thinkers want to get a more complete and accurate picture of the problem before trying to come up with a solution. They don't believe that the cause of a problem is necessarily obvious or quick and easy to find. People, often unintentionally, create or contribute to their own problems and the power and responsibility to change these problems lies within them rather in outside factors.

Systems thinkers know that finding quick fixes to a problem often will either be ineffective or make the problem worse by causing unintended negative consequences. They look to improve the entire system by focusing on and strengthening the relationships between the parts. They believe that focusing on too many strategies at once will scatter focus and won't lead to a lasting change. They would rather focus all of their attention on implementing a few key changes, leverage points, that they believe will impact the whole system. They keep working on the chosen change for a period of time to see if they are effective.

Collective Impact introduced by John Kania and Mark Kramer in the Stanford Social Innovation Review

Social issues are chronic and complex. They have been resistant to a large variety of solutions offered despite the efforts and best intentions of people for many years. Often in frustration, the strategy tends to be one of "if we throw enough at them, something is bound to stick." Quick, scattered fixes have unintended negative consequences and don't support long-term goals.

Collective impact recognizes that we can achieve more working together than we could ever hope to alone. This process, as described by John Kania and Mark Kramer, occurred when a group of community leaders realized that their individual efforts to improve a piece of a local public education system, while good, weren't having nearly as big of an impact as they could if the entire system was changed. That drove this group of leaders to abandon the individual goals of their organizations in favor of joining together and working collectively on one unifying goal of improving student achievement.

Collective impact leads to:

- mutually reinforcing activities

- a common agenda,

- shared measurement,

- continuous communication.[lxv]

Mutually reinforcing activities means that not everyone has to be doing exactly the same thing as everyone has their own strengths that they bring to the table, but everything that is done has to be coordinated and aligned toward achieving the unified purpose. It builds trust because participants assure each other of their best intentions, pledging to do the best they can with what they know at the moment. People are committed to their common purpose. Mutually reinforcing activities help people recognize the unintended negative consequences of their well-intentioned actions. This way people will acknowledge their interdependence on one hand and their individual responsibilities on the other hand. These two realizations may help people work better together, trying to avoid individual mistakes and their impact on the system as a whole.

A common agenda includes a shared vision of change, a shared understanding of the problem and its root cause, including how any of the organizations or individuals within them may have unintentionally contributed to it, and a unified plan of action they will take together to try to solve the problem. It is important to include a realistic view of where the system currently is and *why* it has gotten stuck there. Even in the most inefficiently working systems, there has to be some type of payoff built in that keeps people willing and comfortable to fall back on the status quo instead of pushing forward to a real solution. Being aware of this inbuilt payoff mechanism is an acknowledgement that change is hard and they will have to overcome the old patterns of behavior if they are going to be successful.

The common agenda offers a distinction of the desired goal and the current payoff system. It becomes obvious to the people involved that change comes with a price and possible sacrifices on each side. However, they also get a realistic outlook on what can be expected in the future so that everyone gets on the same page and ready to do their part to close the gap between where they are now and where they want to be.

Shared measurement values both qualitative and quantitative data. Systems thinkers analyze progress on many parallel time-lines, look for both intended and unintended consequences of certain actions, and track performance from the perspective of the real system purpose. David Peter Stroh comes up with the example of shelter beds in homeless shelters to illustrate shared measurement. With systems thinking metrics, our main goal is to eradicate homelessness by focusing on having less shelter beds (short-term solution) and having more permanent housing (long-term solution). Conventional metrics focus on spending funds on more beds to expand shelters to receive more homeless in immediate need.[lxvi]

Continuous communication is key to the success of a collective impact effort. The quality and the consistency of the communication evolve as people get more attached and responsible for a common cause. They will also be able to distinguish better short-term fixes from long-term achievements. Communication by itself is not enough. It is important to learn and update information continuously as the cause evolves so that the communication can be up to date and relevant.

Telling system stories and the iceberg model

Storytelling is a helpful tool we can use to make sense of the world and how we fit in it. Stories are a way to share our experiences with others and let them know who we are and the things that are important to us. Stories can also be a very powerful way to motivate and inspire others and make our message memorable. Storytelling has been used as a way to help people suffering from traumatic events to heal, to help keep the peace between groups humanizing the "enemy," helps politicians connect with voters, and teachers to engage students in the learning material.

In order to tell a system story there must be some shifts in the way people think:

- Their view expands from just seeing their part of the system to seeing more of the system. They understand how and why the system is currently operating as well as what the plan is to change it.

- They move from placing the blame on others and outside forces to accepting personal responsibility for their contribution to the problem and committing to change their behavior to help improve the system.

- They shift their focus from trying to quickly react to immediate problems (school shooting, low-performing stock market) to directing their attention toward understanding the deeper system structures that cause those events to happen.

A system story increases self-awareness. It opens people's eyes to how their actions may have had unintended consequences that contributed to their own problems as well as those of the system. It makes them more proactive. They realize that they already have the power and leverage within them to effect the desired change. They accept personal responsibility for their thoughts and behavior and recognize that they have the power to create the change they want.

The Iceberg Model

When they were on their tragically ill-fated journey, the Titanic could have likely weathered the crash if it were not for the terrible damage caused to it by the massive portion of the iceberg that lay beneath the surface.

This is much the same case when people in a system are faced with a problem. At first glance, when looking at a problem, the concern and immediate focus may be on the tip of the iceberg that they can see: the event. Focus immediately turns to figuring out what happened with the concern being wanting to react to it quickly so that the fire (or ice) can be put out. But if you want to address more than the symptoms, and get to the root cause of the problem in order to prevent it from happening again, you can't spend all of your time near the, dealing with and reacting to the event. You need to dig deeper because that is where the real issues reside, and these shape the events as well as the trends (patterns of behavior over time, which allow us to forecast and predict what might come next).

The iceberg model distinguishes the symptoms and the real problems exposing the underlining systems structures. The structure is where you will find the policies, dynamics of power, perceptions, and purpose. If left unchanged, the structure is where the vast majority of damage to the system will come from as the trends and events will continue to repeat themselves. The deeper your understanding of the system's structure, the more likely you will be to change the system's behavior for the long-term.

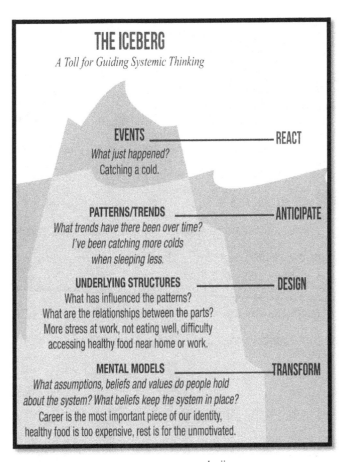

THE ICEBERG

A Toll for Guiding Systemic Thinking

EVENTS ———————————— REACT
What just happened?
Catching a cold.

PATTERNS/TRENDS ——————— ANTICIPATE
What trends have there been over time?
I've been catching more colds
when sleeping less.

UNDERLYING STRUCTURES ————— DESIGN
What has influenced the patterns?
What are the relationships between the parts?
More stress at work, not eating well, difficulty
accessing healthy food near home or work.

MENTAL MODELS ——————— TRANSFORM
What assumptions, beliefs and values do people hold
about the system? What beliefs keep the system in place?
Career is the most important piece of our identity,
healthy food is too expensive, rest is for the unmotivated.

Diagram 17: The Iceberg Model[lxvii]

Let's talk about the levels of the iceberg you can see in diagram 17.

1. The Event Level

People perceive the world at the event level most of the time. For example, waking up in the middle of the night realizing that you're thirsty is an event level analysis. Event level problems can often be solved with a simple correction, like drinking a glass of water. However, the iceberg model encourages us to dig deeper instead of automatically assuming that the problem we are facing is indeed an event level problem. Instead of just reacting to our thirst, let's dig deeper.

2. The Pattern Level

When we look beyond events, we often identify patterns. Events with strong resemblance have been occurring with us over time – we have been very thirsty in differing parts of the day. Maybe we are dangerously dehydrated. Acknowledging patterns helps us forecast and forestall events.

3. The Structure Level

When we try to find the answer to the question, "What's the cause of the pattern we are observing?" we usually conclude that it's some kind of structure. Because of our increased workload in the heat of the day, we often forget to drink enough water and this has taken its toll on our body in the summer heat. Professor John Gerber informs us that structures can include the following things:[lxviii]

> - Physical things — stores, sidewalks, or benches in a park.
>
> - Organizations — corporations, hospitals, and schools.

- Policies — regulations, restrictions, or taxes.

- Rituals — subconscious behaviors.

4. The Mental Model Level

The fourth level of the iceberg are the mental models, which are the collection of the attitudes, beliefs, expectations, morals, and values that provide structures continuous functioning. For example, the beliefs we subconsciously adopt and carry on from home or from our school, work, and surroundings. In the case of our dehydration, the mental model creating it could involve the belief that our job is more important than our health, that we need the money, or that by taking a short drinking break we might appear weak or lazy.[lxix]

Let's carry our iceberg analogy to a specific example of a systemic problem: the reform of the justice system affecting incarceration rates. Between 1960 and 2008 incarceration levels rose by 60% despite a 25% drop in crimes committed. Some people argued that this data showed that locking people up for committing crimes caused the overall crime rate to drop while others thought it was racism and fear that were driving more incarcerations rather than the seriousness of the crime committed.

When people try to find a quick fix to a chronic and complex social problem like criminal justice reform by focusing more on the tip of the iceberg by being most concerned with the latest statistics on crimes committed, repeat offenders, and the costs of the prison system, they miss the big picture and often contribute to negative unintended consequences.

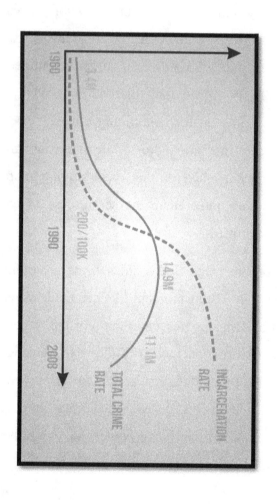

Diagram 18: Crime Rates Versus Incarceration Rates.

The well-intentioned "solution" of issuing harsh sentences to those who commit crimes isn't concerned that people who have been incarcerated have a hard time reentering society after they are released in part because their criminal record discourages future employment opportunities.

Harsh prison sentences don't take into consideration the underlying socioeconomic issues that contribute to the majority of inner city crime. These sentences don't address how difficult it is for people who have been incarcerated to return to become productive members of their community because they are unprepared. They have been emotionally and psychologically hardened by their time in jail and that, coupled with their lack of employment opportunities, contributes to nearly half of them returning to jail for committing a repeat offense within the first three years.[lxx]

The sentences don't address the vacuum left in the communities when the likelihood of the future generation committing crimes increases because the children were left without a high-quality foster care. Or improving the high recidivism rate being due to a lack of unpreparedness of ex-convicts because prisons don't actually reform criminals in anyway. We don't educate them, give them marketable job skills, and then societally we punish them for the crime they commit in perpetuity, which may have been related to say stealing to feed their family, which while not admirable is understandable.

Some countries don't impose death penalties or life sentences, even for the harshest crimes. Let's take Norway as an example. The now thirty-nine year old Anders Behring Breivick murdered seventy-seven people (including children) in 2011. He was sentenced to twenty-one years in prison, which may be prolonged, if deemed required. He lives in conditions described as "a three-room suite with windows, about 340 square feet, that includes a treadmill, a fridge, a DVD player, a Sony PlayStation, and a desk with a typewriter. He has been taking distance-learning courses at his country's main university. He has access to television, radio, and newspapers. He prepares his own food, and he entered the Christmas gingerbread-house baking contest at his prison."[lxxi]

While the case of Andres Behring Breivick is extreme, and clearly shows the unpreparedness of the Norwegian legal system to punish such crimes as he committed, the inmates of Norway do have a mentality that they will go back into society, and reintegrate. They have this mentality because the incarceration in Norway's criminal justice system works on the principle of restorative justice and rehabilitating prisoners. There are correctional facilities in Norway, which make sure that prisoners can become a productive and useful member of the society again. This approach helps Norway maintaining one of the lowest recidivism rates in the world, currently twenty percent, with less than 4000 people in prison, and one of the lowest crime rates in the world.[lxxiilxxiiilxxiv]

Looking at Norway's example, it's clear that, like for many other things in the need for improvement, education is the answer.

The story of balancing feedback loops

Balancing feedback loops are the driving force behind improving a social system because they act to correct the system's behavior by closing the gap between where the system currently is and where we want it to be. Balancing loops operate in equilibrium and are already moving along achieving their goals.

When a balancing feedback loop is achieving its purpose, the corrections it makes can be nearly undetectable, and we tend to take it for granted. When it isn't performing as we expect and meeting its goal, we become aware of it. Balancing feedback loops can help reveal to us why the system is resistant to change.

Corrective action fails to work in the way it was intended for one or more of the following reasons:

- As soon as we think the problem is solved, we stop focusing on the solution and open the door for the problem to come back. An example of this was demonstrated in Boston in the early 1990s. Boston administrators were trying to solve their problem of youth crime in the city. Community and political leaders joined together and coordinated their efforts to solve the problem. They came up with a variety of solutions like after-school programs, community policing, neighborhood watches, and gang outreach, all of which proved to be very successful in reducing youth crime. Thinking that the problem was solved, the political leaders thought they should remove funding from those programs in order to address more urgent concerns. It wasn't long before the problem of youth crime returned.[lxxv]

- We underestimate the amount of time it will take to effect positive lasting change. When change doesn't happen on our time schedule, we tend to either get discouraged and give up too soon or get impatient and push too hard for results before they are ready. Thankfully, a community in Massachusetts was more patient and persistent than most. They were experiencing a problem with high rates of teen and adult drug and alcohol abuse. The community remained committed to their coordinated efforts and after a period of eleven years, they experienced success with their solution for bringing the teen alcohol and drug abuse rates down.

- The system participants are not unified behind a clear-shared vision and purpose. They do not agree on a common understanding of where the system currently is and where it should be. Without a common agenda, there is little hope for coming up with a solution that will effect meaningful and lasting change.

Based on the observations made in the three points above, policy makers can adjust their actions as follows:

- Ensure the reinforcement of the interventions that prove to bring good results instead of reducing support when the problem becomes less pressing.
- Acknowledge the perception, delivery, and adoption delay of the correcting actions. Practice patience and persistence with the interference.

- Before developing an intervention strategy, make sure every actor involved shares the same understanding, goals, and reality.

The story of reinforcing feedback loops: success to the successful

As we discussed in the chapter with the systems archetypes, in case of the "success to the successful" archetype a reinforcing feedback loop is in control. Let's recapitulate the main system story behind this archetype:

- Systems have a finite amount of resources. When one person or group gains an advantage over another in terms of wealth or success, they can use it to gain even more resources. This is not a bad thing by itself but it may lead the other person or group at a disadvantage of allocating resources. That disadvantage grows as time passes because they are less able to get the resources they need to stay competitive. The gap widens over time and it becomes a difficult cycle to break.

- Those who are wealthy have more money to invest in capital like land, equipment, stocks and bonds, and better education and healthcare. This in turn makes them better able to earn more income quickly and accumulate more wealth because their capital allows them to be more productive. The wealthy also have more access to other wealthy and influential people who can offer them greater networking and business opportunities that contribute to their success.

- Those who are not wealthy have to spend more of their money on goods, and they do not have money left over to invest in the capital that would help them generate more wealth. The gap between the haves and have nots continues to widen, and the cycle keeps repeating.

In a social system, reinforcing loops have dynamics that support the majority of wealth and success being concentrated on a small percentage while other dynamics line up against the lower class, and especially minorities, being able to experience comparable levels of success. Keith Lawrence, the co-director of Aspen Institute Roundtable on Community Change calls this phenomenon structural racism. He argues that some dynamics – historical, cultural, institutional and interpersonal - regularly favor white people and exponentially hinder the chances of people of color to succeed. He strengthens his statement by bringing up examples such as gerrymandering, the fact that the majority of incarcerated people are black men.[lxxvi] Children born into less fortunate families start their lives off at a disadvantage because their parents are under great pressure to make ends meet and may not be able to afford high quality health care.

Societies whose main aim is sustainability try to minimize the effects of the "success to the successful" archetype by improving the redistribution system and raising awareness on the structural problems of resource allocations.

Chapter 9: A Comprehensive Study on Systems Thinking and a Social Issue

The story

Calhoun County, Michigan, around Battle Creek with a population of about 100,000 had a chronic social problem of homelessness. Business, political, and community leaders, along with those who were homeless, began asking questions about why, despite their best efforts, they were still unable to end homelessness in their community. They united together along with the Battle Creek Homeless Coalition, determined to find a solution affect positive lasting change. They combined their efforts and used systems thinking to unite behind a purpose and common agenda to create a ten-year plan to eliminate homelessness in their area. They studied data and worked to form a shared vision of where they want to be as well as an honest picture and understanding of where they currently were. They agreed upon the leverage points that they thought would be most effective and helpful in redesigning the system's structure.[lxxvii]

Through their thorough research into the risk factors of homelessness, the four stages of homelessness, why people end up on the streets only temporarily, and by conducting many interviews with people in their community, they identified their major concern of the difficulty of moving people from temporary homeless shelters into safe, affordable, supportive, permanent housing.

The homelessness has four stages:

- People becoming at risk of losing their homes
- People losing their homes and having to live on the streets
- People finding temporary shelter off the streets
- People moving from temporary shelter back into permanent housing"[lxxviii]

The Battle Creek Homeless Coalition identified some barriers to their success: providing government subsidies to help keep people in their own homes, getting the entire community – schools, churches, families, and friends – involved in offering their support, informing people of the community assistance and programs that were

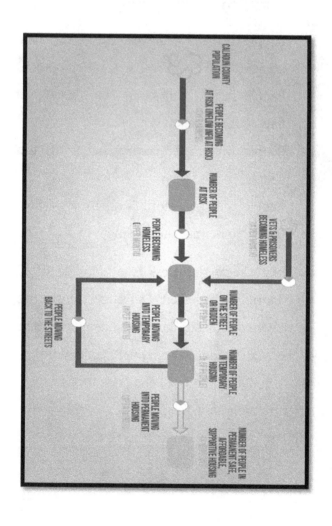

Diagram 19: The Four Stages Of Homelessness.[lxxix]

available to them, and enlisting the help of the Veteran's Administration to offer help to veterans were good steps, but weren't enough to sustain the solution in the long run on their own.

They also were aware that they didn't want to fall back into the old habits of relying on temporary shelters because they helped to hide the problem and reduce the sense of urgency. They also offered short-term success, which pleased people donating to the cause. The donors chose to financially support individual organizations which caused them to take their focus away from the big picture and compete with each other for resources instead.

This quick fix to address a symptom didn't get to the root of the problem of homelessness and caused unintended negative consequences as it helped to create a dependence on, or addiction to, the temporary homeless shelters.

The Battle Creek Homeless Coalition identified seven leverage points that they felt would give them the most "bang for their buck" in changing the system as a whole. They grouped them according to whether they were designed to reduce the inflow into shelters by keeping people who were at risk of becoming homeless or increase the outflow by getting more people to move out of the temporary shelters and into permanent housing quickly.

After all of their intensive study, they found that the cheapest leverage points to implement were those that kept people in their own homes and prevented them from becoming homeless in the first place. They coordinated their efforts into increasing affordable housing by supporting landlords who were willing to rent to people who are at risk. They tried to create additional better paying jobs so that people at risk could afford their rent payments. They also provided integrated community services designed to give people the support they needed to stay in their homes.[lxxx]

Results

Were their efforts successful? During the first three years of implementing their plan, from 2007-2009, homelessness decreased by 13% and eviction rates dropped by 3%. This was in spite of the recession our country was in that spurred a 70% increase in unemployment and a 15% increase in people filing for bankruptcy in Calhoun County.[lxxxi]

The Coordinating Council of Calhoun County reported that in 2016, there were 1,190 people who were considered "literally homeless," which means that they were either living in a public or private shelter or in a public or private place not intended for human habitation. Based on this data and the new regulations in the county, they are on track to potentially reduce homelessness by 28% in 9 years. System changes don't happen overnight, but the fact that homelessness is on the decline by a significant percentage in Calhoun County is promising progress.[lxxxii]

The four stages of change based on the homeless story

Author David Peter Stroh identifies four stages of change. Stroh, quoting Peter Sange, the author of the book *The Fifth Discipline*, describes social changes as such, "the energy for change is mobilized by establishing a discrepancy between what people want and where they are. (…) When people have a common aspiration – as expressed by a shared vision, mission, and set of values – and a shared understanding of not only where they are now but also why – then they establish creative tension, which they are drawn to resolve in favor of their aspiration."[lxxxiii]

Creating a shared understanding is crucial to seeing why the current problems exist and what can be the best solutions to it that are more than quick fixes. For example, they will see how the pressure to build a new homeless shelter is only a Band-Aid™ to the problem. Homelessness will persist and so will their dependence on the shelters.

The shared picture will help people to commit to the idea "I will get my part done, and I'll make sure we all get the whole thing done." The creative tension rooting in the shared picture, brings forth the idea of the four stages of change. Let's go through these stages one by one.

1. Stage 1 – This is where the foundation of the change is built. In the case of our story, stage one occurred when the Battle Creek Homeless Coalition and the homeless people, asked for the input of business, political, and community leaders of Calhoun County. They met and started asking hard questions about why they still had a problem with homelessness despite their best efforts and decided that they

were all ready to make a change. These stakeholders were actively engaged in coming up with a common agenda in which they agreed upon their shared view of where they would like for the system to be. They cultivated a shared vision of what successful change would look like and set their common purpose. They learned how to effectively communicate with each other.

2. Stage 2 – This is the "reality check" stage where they gathered and organized information to help give them a clear and honest picture of where the system was currently. They did interviews and looked back in history to see if the system had been there before. Then they organized the information they had gathered to

develop a basic system analysis on how the different actors had interacted over time to help or deter the common goal. They formed a shared view of what was happening and began to analyze *why* it was happening. They accepted responsibility for any role they may have played in contributing to the problem.

3. Stage 3 – This is a "tell it like it is" stage. At this stage, people have to face the facts that change is hard and things might have to get worse before they get better. It is in this stage that they acknowledge that even in a flawed system there is some benefit that people are getting from it or the system wouldn't be stuck where it was.

   Real and lasting change takes a significant investment of time, effort, money, and resources. It requires commitment and sacrifice on the part of everyone involved.

This stage is where people recognize that they will need to resist the temptation of giving in to quick fixes and short term solutions and stick with the plan for the long haul. They have to weigh the benefits and sacrifices that will accompany change and the costs of not acting and just maintaining the system's current status. Hard trade offs, delayed gratification, temporary back fall should all be accepted side effects of the change. Then they need to make a conscious choice to buy in fully to the purpose and commit to being part of the solution.

In our story, this was where the Battle Creek Homeless Coalition reached a crucial turning point in their development of a solution because they realized the system was currently helping people cope with homelessness by providing them with shelters, but that was ultimately undermining their purpose of ending homelessness.

4. Stage 4 – This is the stage where people bridge the gap between where the system currently is and where they want it to be. In this stage they identify the leverage points they believe will be most helpful in effecting change. They commit to continuous learning and agree to meet to update and adjust their plan and goals if the data they are receiving warrants it in order to stay on

track and focused on achieving their unified purpose.

In the case of our story, the leverage points they selected served as the goals for their ten-year plan. When they began to get a handle on what was working and where they had some needs that others could help meet, they reached out to bring in and engage new stakeholders. They brought in people who could help with economic development in creating new better paying jobs, people with ideas and resources for increasing affordable housing, and people with experience in foster care and the criminal justice system.

These stages are an ongoing circular process. What they learn in Stage 4 gives feedback to Stage 1 again and the process continues.

Chapter 10: Exercises

This chapter will lay out some exercises that can be helpful for teambuilding and getting the systems thinking juices flowing as you begin to work on analyzing a system's problems and generating a lasting and meaningful solution.

A Warm up exercise

This icebreaker is a good way to start a meeting where the goal is to challenge people's creativity and inner idea machine.

Time:

About 5 minutes.

Instructions:

Explain this as an exercise to practice mental agility before beginning the meeting. Ask participants to follow your instructions mentally. Speak slowly and pause between each instruction:

1) choose a number from 1 to 9

2) subtract 5

3) multiply it by 3

4) square the number (multiply by the same number-- not square root)

5) add the digits together until you get only one digit (i.e. 64=6+4= 10 = 1+0=1)

6) if the number is less than 5, add five - otherwise subtract 4.

7) multiply it by 2

8) subtract 6

9) match the digit to a letter in the alphabet 1=A, 2=B, 3=C, etc...

10) choose the name of a country that begins with that letter

11) take the second letter in the country's name and think of an animal that begins with that letter

12) think of the color of that animal

Results:

Chances are you thought of a grey or pink elephant from Denmark. Why?

The number trick gives you a "4" every time, which means you always think of a "D." The countries that start with the letter "D" are Denmark, Djibouti and the Dominican Republic. Djibouti deserves a 1% chance if you happen to come from there or the area. So does the Dominican Republic. But let's be real, it's not surprising that most people think of Denmark.[lxxxiv]

What if we indeed picked Djibouti? We'd get animals like jaguars, jackals, jackrabbits, or jellyfish. If we picked Dominican Republic we'd come up with an octopus, otter, owl, ostrich, or one of many other possibilities. Since we picked Denmark, our animal name had to begin with an "e." If you chose elephant you picked the most common answer and likely the first one that popped into your head.

Keep in mind when we are content to pick the quick and/or popular answer that means most other people, including our competitors, are coming up with the same answer too. Let's spend time looking for something beyond the most obvious thought. Here are some animals that begin with the letter "e:"

- eagles
- earless seals
- earthworms
- earwigs
- echidnas
- elephant beetles
- emperor moths

- emperor penguins
- emydid turtles
- engraver beetles
- ensign wasp.

Do you have any questions left?

Playing and Designing a Game

Choose a well-known board game. Review the rules of the game with the participants, and then make a group decision to change the rules. Ask each person to make one change to the rules by changing, adding, or eliminating one of the original rules. Play the new version of the game created collectively by the group. Ask the following questions for discussion:

> 1. What does having a set of rules tell us about how a system works?
> 2. What's the difference between playing and designing a game?
> 3. What is different about the system when the game is being played and when it is being designed?

Results:

This activity is presented in a fun game format, but it provides a good opportunity to compare and contrast playing and designing. When we play a game, our focus is on taking turns as we follow the rules that were laid out for us and try to win. In contrast, designing the game involves not only playing it, but it also requires a higher level thinking skill of reflecting upon the possible changes you might make and the consequences that will result because of those changes.

Designing requires an understanding of the holistic and systemic view of the game. When you design a game, you make decisions based on who the target audience is. That's why we have different games and different rules. We use the same tools tailored for different people, such as children, and different purposes, such as whether it is intended to teach a skill or it is just to be played for fun. We can discover the rules and variations through repeated occasions of playing the same game. It is from experiences like these that we can gain a deeper understanding of the meaning of being part of a system. It is through collective activities such as these that the group becomes a more visible and real human social system.[lxxxv]

From *Seven Activities to Engage Systems Thinking* by Arne Collen & Gianfranco Minati

A Language Game

The game is best played with another person whose primary language is your secondary language. Choose a word or phrase from your primary language and translate it into your secondary language. For example, if English is your primary language, you might translate the words into Spanish as your second language. You would then ask the person you are playing with to translate the Spanish back into English. Continue taking turns back and forth in this manner until each person has completed several words or phrases. Observe the differences in meaning between the original words of the primary speaker and those translated back in a secondary language. Ask the following questions for discussion:

1. How is language important in a living system?

2. What can happen when two systems, that have different languages, must communicate?

3. What problems can arise when two systems with different languages try to communicate?

4. What solutions might be helpful to address the problems that can arise when two systems with difference languages need to communicate?

There is a move to help people communicate across different languages by using Artificial Intelligence. This can solve some problems with communication, but there is also the potential for some meaning to be lost by having a computer translate. In order to avoid this, there is recognition that translation does require input from a human being and translations always have an author and are copyrighted. As we become more and more connected in our world today, our extensive global communications network has become a system of its own complete with interconnected and interdependent languages as subsystems. We need to be respectful, tolerant, and appreciative of diversity. We should be open to the possibility of learning from language and cultures that are quite different from our own and be kind and ethical global citizens.[lxxxvi]

From *Seven Activities to Engage Systems Thinking* by Arne Collen & Gianfranco Minati

SPOT

This exercise works best with groups of less than ten people. Some people will not fall into the trap but most will. The idea is not to trick or embarrass people but rather to get everyone laughing together. This can be used to spark discussions about the power of mindfulness and how it helps us to think systemically.

Time:

About 5 minutes.

Instructions:

Quickly ask an individual or small group the following questions. Only pause briefly to allow a response and ask them to answer in a loud energetic voice:

1. Ask them to say the word SPOT three times as quickly as they can

2. Ask them to spell the word SPOT once

3.   Now ask them what they do when they come to a green light

Results: Many people will say STOP, a few will say GO. If you ask them the question again, many will repeat the same answer and possibly get defensive about their answer being right.

You could then ask them "How many of you drove to work today? What did you do when you came to a green light?" and joke that you could've asked them what they do when they get to a red light but you suspect that if they're anything like a lot of other drivers in your town they would probably run through it.

We live in a society that often expects people to give answers as quickly as possible. There is comfort in numbers so when we hear others saying the same answer we are giving it makes us feel more confident that we are right. While it is good to allow ourselves to fall into patterns (they are healthy signs), sometimes we need to slow down and check our answers to be sure we are giving the correct ones.[lxxxvii]

From *The Systems Thinking Playbook* by Linda Booth Sweeney & Dennis Meadows

Simon Says

This exercise can be used to give the group a chance to walk around a little and stretch after a long period of sitting, or to serve as a fun and gentle reminder that we can all benefit from listening a little more carefully.

Time:

About 5 minutes.

Instructions:

Introduce this activity as a chance for the participants to experience the latest test that the police are giving when they pull drivers over to check for drinking and driving.

1. Stand up, get in front of the participants and ask them to stand up too. Explain to them that in this activity they have to do what you **tell them** to do.

2. Ask them to stretch both of their arms out at shoulder height (as you say it do it as well)

3. Ask them to make a circle with the thumb and index finger of their right hand (you do it as you are saying it)

4. Ask them to take their thumb and index finger (still in the circle), and put the circle on their cheek **(you will put your thumb and index finger on your chin instead)**

Results:

Most people will have put their thumb and index finger on their chin instead of on their cheek because most people will have followed your actions instead of your words.

It is important that we follow through with our actions to support what we have said we will do.[lxxxviii]

From *The Systems Thinking Playbook* by Linda Booth Sweeney & Dennis Meadows

Conclusion

Systems thinking is a powerful lens through which we can see the world and analyze the systems within it. We have discussed what a crucial impact it has on our ability to make well-informed objective decisions based on evidence and data, get to the root of and solve even the most challenging complex and chronic problems, and create a strategic plan of the highest quality that works to focus and align everyone's efforts on the system's unifying purpose.

Here is just a small sampling of things we can accomplish by using systems thinking:

- See the big picture (the whole system) more clearly

- Discover and accept responsibility for the unintended negative consequences that we may have inadvertently contributed through our actions

- Develop solutions that are beneficial to the entire system and effect lasting and meaningful change

- Avoid quick fixes that ultimately can make things worse in the long term

- Increase our understanding of the problems we are trying to solve

- Create a strategic plan complete with leverage points that make the best possible use of available resources

- Predict and avoid the unintended negative consequences that may arise from proposed solutions

- View learning as a worthwhile and continuous process

- Commit to doing our part by not only improving our part of the system, but working to improve the entire system
- Recognize that our individual and collective thinking impacts the results we achieve

Systems thinking is a paradigm shift in which we move from placing blame on people and things we can't control to accepting responsibility and empowering ourselves to take control of our own reality. It is a shift from being so emotionally attached to our own beliefs and clinging to them at all costs, assuming that we must be right, to being humble and open to the ideas and beliefs of others. It involves accepting the fact that we aren't always right and that we have plenty we can learn from others. It is being willing to expand our perspective and abandon or adapt our beliefs when presented with evidence that warrants it.

Strong systems thinkers subscribe to the core principles of how systems work:

- **Feedback:** the way a system performs is closely tied to the circular, interconnected relationships within it.

- **Growth & Stability:** Feedback loops show us how systems grow (reinforcing loops) or remain stable (equilibrium caused by balancing loops).

- **Diversity & Resilience:** Diversity allows systems to grow while resilience keeps systems stable when change occurs.

- **Delay:** Our choices and actions result in consequences which can be immediate or delayed.

- **Power of Awareness:** When we take a good, hard, honest look at where a system is currently operating, we can build upon its strengths and work to overcome its weaknesses.

- **Unintended Consequences:** It is quite possible that the challenges we are facing today are a result of a solution we instituted in the past.

- **Leverage:** Meaningful and lasting change within a system occurs when we focus on implementing a few key coordinated changes and sustain them over a period of time.

Understanding these core principles is key to helping us recognize patterns in system behavior so we can create a strategic plan aimed at achieving the system's purpose.

Donella Meadows explained "Social systems are the external manifestations of cultural thinking patterns and of profound human needs, emotions, strengths, and weaknesses."[lxxxix] In order to be effective in bringing about social change, we have to strengthen our systems thinking skills.

While we often think of our cognitive abilities as the key to systems thinking, strong systems thinkers also work to develop themselves in emotional, behavioral, physical, and spiritual areas. Being well-rounded and integrating all areas of life in decision making makes us better prepared and more efficient in using systems thinking to face the difficult challenges we wish to overcome.

Becoming a systems thinker takes practice. There will be times when you will need to seek guidance and help from others and times when you get stuck because the task seems insurmountable. It is then that you should rely on one of the most important skills systems thinkers have – the ability to ask great questions. When we ask the right questions, we open ourselves up to new ways of thinking, communicating, and understanding. Here are examples of a few powerful questions:

- Why are we unable to achieve our goal despite our best efforts and intentions?

- What responsibility do we bear for the problems we are facing?

- How can we create common ground among our stakeholders?

- What sacrifices will we need to make to enable the system as a whole to succeed?

- What might the unintended consequences of this possible solution be?

It is important for systems thinkers to view themselves as works in progress. There is always new knowledge to be gained and always room to learn, grow, and improve. There are some characteristics that are helpful to try to cultivate within ourselves; some of these are curiosity, respect, and compassion.[xc]

Systems thinking gives us the tools and skills we need to be able to take a complex, and sometimes chronic problem, improve our shared understanding of it, and align and organize the pieces into a clear roadmap of the path we should take in order to redesign the system's structure and achieve its purpose.

Systems thinking is in large part about connections: making, recognizing, understanding, and strengthening them. When we understand that everything in a system is connected and we cultivate and nurture the positive connections while working to diminish and remove the dysfunctional ones, it isn't long until we have the pieces of the system working together in harmony, united in service to the whole, and trying to contribute to the greater good. And what could be better than that?

Reference

Books and printed papers:

Beresford-Jones, D., S. Arce, O.Q. Whaley and A. Chepstow-Lusty. The Role of Prosopis in Ecological and Landscape Change in the Samaca Basin, Lower Ica Valley, South Coast Peru from the Early Horizon to the Late Intermediate Period. Latin American Antiquity Vol. 20 pp. 303–330. 2009.

Booth Sweeney, Linda. Meadows, Dennis. The Systems Thinking Playbook. Chelsea Green Publishing. 2010.

Forrester, Jay. Collected Papers of Jay Forrester. Jay Forrester. Pegasus Communications. 1975.

Frey, Rebecca Joyce. Genocide and International Justice. Facts On File. ISBN 978-0816073108. 2009.

Geoff W Adams, The Emperor Commodus : gladiator, Hercules or a tyrant?. Boca Raton: BrownWalker Press. ISBN 1612337228. 2013.

Meadows, Donella. Thinking in Systems: A primer. Chelsea Green Publishing. 2008.

Seonmin Kim, Victoria Jane Mabin, John Davies. The theory of constraints thinking processes: retrospect and prospect. International Journal of

Operations & Production Management, Vol. 28
Issue: 2, pp.155-184. 2008.
https://doi.org/10.1108/01443570810846883

Silverman Helaine. Proulx ,Donald A. The Nasca.
Blackwell Publishers. Malden. 2002.

Stroh, Peter David. Systems Thinking For Social
Change. Chelsea Green Publishing. 2015.

Von Bertalanffy, Ludwig. An Outline of General
System Theory. The British Journal for the
Philosophy of Science, Vol. 1, No. 2, pp. 134-165.
1950.

Online Articles and studies:

Aronson, Daniel. Overview of Systems Thinking. Daniel Aronson. 1996. http://www.thinking.net/Systems_Thinking/OverviewSTarticle.pdf

Battle Creek Michigan. Homeless Coalition discusses local facts on health fair day. Battle Creek Michigan. 2017. https://www.battlecreekmi.gov/CivicAlerts.aspx?AID=505&ARC=624

Beattie, Andrwe. Why Buying in Bulk Doesn't Always Save You Money. Investopedia. 2018. https://www.investopedia.com/articles/pf/07/bulk_buying.asp

Bregel, Emily. Fog-induced wreck prompted lawsuits. Times Free Press. 2010. https://www.timesfreepress.com/news/news/story/

2010/dec/05/fog-induced-wreck-prompted-lawsuits/36307/

Chatteerjee, Pratap. Dick Cheney's Halliburton: a corporate case study. The Guardian. 2011. https://www.theguardian.com/commentisfree/cifamerica/2011/jun/08/dick-cheney-halliburton-supreme-court

Collaboration for Impact. The Collective Impact Framework. Collaboration for Impact. 2018. https://www.collaborationforimpact.com/collective-impact/

Collen, Arne. Minati, Gianfranco. Seven Activities To Engage Systems Thinking. Semantic Scholar. 1997. https://pdfs.semanticscholar.org/3436/c52688ab6dae545fdb783bb0b88b8b052c16.pdf

Darling-Hammond, Linda. Inequality in Teaching and Schooling: How Opportunity Is Rationed to Students of Color in America NCBI. 2001. https://www.ncbi.nlm.nih.gov/books/NBK223640/

Death Penalty Information Center. Deterrence: States Without the Death Penalty Have Had Consistently Lower Murder Rates. Death Penalty Information Center. 2017. https://deathpenaltyinfo.org/deterrence-states-without-death-penalty-have-had-consistently-lower-murder-rates

Durose, Matthew. Cooper, Alexia D. Ph.D., Snyder, Howard N. Ph.D. Recidivism of Prisoners Released in 30 States in 2005: Patterns from 2005 to 2010. U.S. Department of Justice. 2014.

https://www.bjs.gov/content/pub/pdf/rprts05p0510.pdf

Gav, Big. Norman Borlaug: Saint Or Sinner? Resilience. 2009. https://www.resilience.org/stories/2009-10-01/norman-borlaug-saint-or-sinner/

Gerber, John. Systems Thinking Tools: Finding The Root Cause(S) Of Big Problems. Changing The Story. 2012. https://changingthestory.net/2012/07/18/rootcaus/

Hale, David M. Behind the bling: The story of Clemson's epic championship rings. ESPN. 2017. http://www.espn.com/college-football/story/_/id/20466841/clemson-tigers-dabo-swinney-big-business-college-football-championship-rings

Herbert, Christopher E. Haurin , Donald R. Rosenthal, Stuart S. Duda, Mark. Homeownership Gaps Among Low-Income and Minority Borrowers and Neighborhoods. U.S. Department of Housing and Urban Development. 2005. https://www.huduser.gov/Publications/pdf/Homeo wnershipGapsAmongLow-IncomeAndMinority.pdf

Integrated Taxonomy Information System. https://www.itis.gov

Invasive Animals CRC. Introduction of the cane toad to Australia. Pest Smart. 2012. https://www.pestsmart.org.au/pestsmart-case-study-introduction-of-the-cane-toad-to-australia/

I See Systems. Applying Systems Thinking and Common Archetypes to Organizational Issues. Module 6: Systems Archetypes. 2018.

https://www.iseesystems.com/Online_training/course/module6/6-02-0-0-what.htm

I See Systems. Original picture from Applying Systems Thinking and Common Archetypes to Organizational Issues. Module 6: Systems Archetypes. Implications & Leverage Points. Escalation. I See Systems. 2018. https://www.iseesystems.com/Online_training/course/module6/6-11-3-0-escalimp.htm

I See Systems. Applying Systems Thinking and Common Archetypes to Organizational Issues. Module 6: Systems Archetypes. Implications & Leverage Points. Shifting the Burden. I See Systems. 2018. https://www.iseesystems.com/Online_training/course/module6/6-06-3-0-shiftimp.htm

I See Systems. Applying Systems Thinking and Common Archetypes to Organizational Issues.

Module 6: Systems Archetypes. Implications &
Leverage Points. Success to the Successful. I See
Systems. 2018.

https://www.iseesystems.com/Online_training/cou
rse/module6/6-13-3-0-successimp.htm

Johnston, Ian. Pesticides linked to 'large-scale
population extinctions' of wild beesIndependent.
2016.

https://www.independent.co.uk/news/science/inse
cticides-bees-population-extinction-link-farmers-
toxic-neonicotinoid-oilseed-rape-a7193951.html

Karash, Richard. Mental Models And Systems
Thinking: Going Deeper Into Systemic Issues. The
Systems Thinker. 2018.

https://thesystemsthinker.com/mental-models-and-
systems-thinking-going-deeper-into-systemic-
issues/

Karash, Richard. Goodman, Michael R. Going Deeper: Moving from Understanding to Action. Applied Systems Thinking. 1995. http://www.appliedsystemsthinking.com/supporting_documents/PracticeGoingDeeper.pdf

Kubish C, Anne. Structural Racism. Racial Equity Tools. 2006. www.racialequitytools.org/resourcefiles/kubisch.pdf

Kushinka, Matthew. Countries That Start with D: There's Something Rotten in America. Red Lines. 2018. https://www.redlinels.com/countries-start-d/

Lynn, Bryan. Many US States Struggle with Teacher Shortages. Learning English. 2018. https://learningenglish.voanews.com/a/many-us-

states-struggle-with-teacher-
shortages/4537983.html

Martin, Will. The 31 safest countries in the world.
Business Insider. 2018.
https://www.businessinsider.my/safest-countries-
in-the-world-2018-6/?r=US&IR=T

Merritt, Jeremy. What Are Mental Models? The
Systems Thinker. 2018.
https://thesystemsthinker.com/what-are-mental-
models/

Newswire. Ramapough Mountain Indians Sue
Ford Over Toxic Contamination. Newswire. 2006.
http://www.ens-newswire.com/ens/jan2006/2006-
01-21-01.html

Northwest Earth Institute. A Systems Thinking
Model: The Iceberg. Northwest Earth Institute.
2018. https://www.nwei.org/iceberg/

Onda, Tsuyoshi. Abortion Worldwide 2017:
Uneven Progress and Unequal Access.
Guttmacher. 2018.
https://www.guttmacher.org/report/abortion-
worldwide-2017

Pilkington, Ed. Robin Wright targets Congo's
'conflict minerals' violence with new campaign.
The Guardian. 2016.
https://www.theguardian.com/world/2016/may/17/
robin-wright-stand-with-congo-campaign-mining-
house-of-cards

Pryser Libell, Henrik. Anders Behring Breivik,
Killer in 2011 Norway Massacre, Says Prison
Conditions Violate His Rights. The New York

Times. 2016.
https://www.nytimes.com/2016/03/16/world/europe/anders-breivik-nazi-prison-lawsuit.html

Sherwell, Philip. A plague of Burmese pythons in the Everglades. The Telegraph. 2009.
https://www.telegraph.co.uk/news/worldnews/northamerica/usa/5956739/A-plague-of-Burmese-pythons-in-the-Everglades.html

Sterbenz, Christina. Why Norway's prison system is so successful. Business Insider. 2014.
https://www.businessinsider.com/why-norways-prison-system-is-so-successful-2014-12/?IR=T

Stroh, Peter David. Goodman, Michael. A Systemic Approach to Ending Homelessness. Applied Systems Thinking. 2007.

http://www.appliedsystemsthinking.com/supportin
g_documents/TopicalHomelessness.pdf

Stover, Del. Addressing teacher turnover in high-
poverty, high-minority urban schools. NSBA.
2017.
https://www.nsba.org/newsroom/addressing-
teacher-turnover-high-poverty-high-minority-
urban-schools

Strachan, Glenn. Systems Thinking. International
Research Institute in Sustainability, University of
Gloucestershire. 2018.
http://arts.brighton.ac.uk/__data/assets/pdf_file/00
04/5926/Systems-Thinking.pdf

The Associated Press. Louisiana school has
rescinded its hair extension ban after outcry,
archdiocese says. CBC. 2018.

https://www.cbc.ca/news/world/black-girl-hair-school-policy-extensions-1.4801371

The Nobel Prize. Norman E. Borlaug. The Nobel Prize. 2018.
https://www.nobelprize.org/prizes/peace/1970/borlaug/symposia/

Volz, Matt. Fired pregnant teacher settles with Montana Catholic school. The Boston Globe. 2016.
https://www.bostonglobe.com/news/nation/2016/03/15/fired-pregnant-teacher-settles-with-montana-catholic-school/ShlqaNHnaXXWO2HVUcDxiM/story.html

Von Bertalanffy, Ludwig. The Theory of Open Systems in Physics and Biology Science New Series, Vol. 111, No. 2872 (Jan. 13, 1950), pp. 23-

29 Published by: American Association for the Advancement of Science Stable URL: https://www.jstor.org/stable/1676073

World Prison Brief. Highest to Lowest. Prison Population Total. World Prison Brief. 2018. http://www.prisonstudies.org/highest-to-lowest/prison-population-total?field_region_taxonomy_tid=All

Zurcher, Kathleen. Stroh, Peter David. Acting and Thinking Systemically. The Systems Thinker. 2018. https://thesystemsthinker.com/acting-and-thinking-systemically/

Endnotes

[i] Silverman Helaine. Proulx ,Donald A. The Nasca. Blackwell Publishers. Malden. 2002.

[ii] Beresford-Jones, D., S. Arce, O.Q. Whaley and A. Chepstow-Lusty. The Role of Prosopis in Ecological and Landscape Change in the Samaca Basin, Lower Ica Valley, South Coast Peru from the Early Horizon to the Late Intermediate Period. Latin American Antiquity Vol. 20 pp. 303–330. 2009.

[iii] The Nobel Prize. Norman E. Borlaug. The Nobel Prize. 2018. https://www.nobelprize.org/prizes/peace/1970/borlaug/symposia/

[iv] Johnston, Ian. Pesticides linked to 'large-scale population extinctions' of wild beesIndependent. 2016. https://www.independent.co.uk/news/science/insecticides-bees-population-extinction-link-farmers-toxic-neonicotinoid-oilseed-rape-a7193951.html

[v] Gav, Big. Norman Borlaug: Saint Or Sinner? Resilience. 2009. https://www.resilience.org/stories/2009-10-01/norman-borlaug-saint-or-sinner/

[vi] Von Bertalanffy, Ludwig. An Outline of General System Theory. The British Journal for the Philosophy of Science, Vol. 1, No. 2, pp. 134-165. 1950.

[vii] Von Bertalanffy, Ludwig. An Outline of General System Theory. The British Journal for the Philosophy of Science, Vol. 1, No. 2, pp. 134-165. 1950.

[viii] Von Bertalanffy, Ludwig. An Outline of General System Theory. The British Journal for the Philosophy of Science, Vol. 1, No. 2, pp. 134-165. 1950.

[ix] Meadows, Donella. Thinking in Systems: A primer. Chelsea Green Publishing. 2008.

[x] Lynn, Bryan. Many US States Struggle with Teacher Shortages. Learning English. 2018.
https://learningenglish.voanews.com/a/many-us-states-struggle-with-teacher-shortages/4537983.html

[xi] Darling-Hammond, Linda. Inequality in Teaching and Schooling: How Opportunity Is Rationed to Students of Color in America NCBI. 2001.
https://www.ncbi.nlm.nih.gov/books/NBK223640/

[xii] Stover, Del. Addressing teacher turnover in high-poverty, high-minority urban schools. NSBA. 2017.
https://www.nsba.org/newsroom/addressing-teacher-turnover-high-poverty-high-minority-urban-schools

[xiii] Volz, Matt. Fired pregnant teacher settles with Montana Catholic school. The Boston Globe. 2016.
https://www.bostonglobe.com/news/nation/2016/03/15/fired-pregnant-teacher-settles-with-montana-catholic-school/ShlqaNHnaXXWO2HVUcDxiM/story.html

[xiv] The Associated Press. Louisiana school has rescinded its hair extension ban after outcry, archdiocese says. CBC. 2018.
https://www.cbc.ca/news/world/black-girl-hair-school-policy-extensions-1.4801371

[xv] Meadows, Donella. Thinking in Systems: A primer. Chelsea Green Publishing. 2008.

[xvi] Von Bertalanffy, Ludwig. The Theory of Open Systems in Physics and Biology Science New Series, Vol. 111, No. 2872 (Jan. 13, 1950), pp. 23-29 Published by: American Association for the Advancement of Science Stable URL: https://www.jstor.org/stable/1676073

[xvii] Merritt, Jeremy. What Are Mental Models? The Systems Thinker. 2018. https://thesystemsthinker.com/what-are-mental-models/

[xviii] Seonmin Kim, Victoria Jane Mabin, John Davies. The theory of constraints thinking processes: retrospect and prospect. International Journal of Operations & Production Management, Vol. 28 Issue: 2, pp.155-184. 2008. https://doi.org/10.1108/01443570810846883

[xix] Karash, Richard. Mental Models And Systems Thinking: Going Deeper Into Systemic Issues. The Systems Thinker. 2018. https://thesystemsthinker.com/mental-models-and-systems-thinking-going-deeper-into-systemic-issues/

[xx] Karash, Richard. Mental Models And Systems Thinking: Going Deeper Into Systemic Issues. The Systems Thinker. 2018. https://thesystemsthinker.com/mental-models-and-systems-thinking-going-deeper-into-systemic-issues/

[xxi] *Diagram 7*. Original picture from Karash, Richard. Mental Models And Systems Thinking: Going Deeper Into Systemic Issues. The Systems Thinker. 2018. https://thesystemsthinker.com/mental-models-and-systems-thinking-going-deeper-into-systemic-issues/

[xxii] Karash, Richard. Mental Models And Systems Thinking: Going Deeper Into Systemic Issues. The

Systems Thinker. 2018.
https://thesystemsthinker.com/mental-models-and-systems-thinking-going-deeper-into-systemic-issues/
[xxiii] Karash, Richard. Goodman, Michael R. Going Deeper: Moving from Understanding to Action. Applied Systems Thinking. 1995.
http://www.appliedsystemsthinking.com/supporting_documents/PracticeGoingDeeper.pdf
[xxiv] Newswire. Ramapough Mountain Indians Sue Ford Over Toxic Contamination. Newswire. 2006.
http://www.ens-newswire.com/ens/jan2006/2006-01-21-01.html
[xxv] Bregel, Emily. Fog-induced wreck prompted lawsuits. Times Free Press. 2010.
https://www.timesfreepress.com/news/news/story/2010/dec/05/fog-induced-wreck-prompted-lawsuits/36307/
[xxvi] Strachan, Glenn. Systems Thinking. International Research Institute in Sustainability, University of Gloucestershire. 2018.
http://arts.brighton.ac.uk/__data/assets/pdf_file/0004/5926/Systems-Thinking.pdf
[xxvii] Invasive Animals CRC. Introduction of the cane toad to Australia. Pest Smart. 2012.
https://www.pestsmart.org.au/pestsmart-case-study-introduction-of-the-cane-toad-to-australia/
[xxviii] Sherwell, Philip. A plague of Burmese pythons in the Everglades. The Telegraph. 2009.
https://www.telegraph.co.uk/news/worldnews/northamerica/usa/5956739/A-plague-of-Burmese-pythons-in-the-Everglades.html
[xxix] Meadows, Donella. Thinking in Systems: A primer. Chelsea Green Publishing. 2008.
[xxx] Frey, Rebecca Joyce. Genocide and International Justice. Facts On File. ISBN 978-0816073108. 2009.

[xxxi] Pilkington, Ed. Robin Wright targets Congo's 'conflict minerals' violence with new campaign. The Guardian. 2016. https://www.theguardian.com/world/2016/may/17/robin-wright-stand-with-congo-campaign-mining-house-of-cards

[xxxii] Integrated Taxonomy Information System. https://www.itis.gov

[xxxiii] Geoff W Adams, The Emperor Commodus : gladiator, Hercules or a tyrant?. Boca Raton: BrownWalker Press. ISBN 1612337228. 2013.

[xxxiv] Aronson, Daniel. Overview of Systems Thinking. Daniel Aronson. 1996. http://www.thinking.net/Systems_Thinking/OverviewSTarticle.pdf

[xxxv] Aronson, Daniel. Overview of Systems Thinking. Daniel Aronson. 1996. http://www.thinking.net/Systems_Thinking/OverviewSTarticle.pdf

[xxxvi] Diagram 8. Original picture from Aronson, Daniel. Overview of Systems Thinking. Daniel Aronson. 1996. Retrieved in 2018. http://www.thinking.net/Systems_Thinking/OverviewSTarticle.pdf

[xxxvii] Diagram 9. Original picture from Aronson, Daniel. Overview of Systems Thinking. Daniel Aronson. 1996. http://www.thinking.net/Systems_Thinking/OverviewSTarticle.pdf

[xxxviii] Aronson, Daniel. Overview of Systems Thinking. Daniel Aronson. 1996. http://www.thinking.net/Systems_Thinking/OverviewSTarticle.pdf

[xxxix] Meadows, Donella. Thinking in Systems: A primer. Chelsea Green Publishing. 2008.

[xl] Forrester, Jay. Collected Papers of Jay Forrester. Jay Forrester. Pegasus Communications. 1975.

[xli] Meadows, Donella. Thinking in Systems: A primer. Chelsea Green Publishing. 2008.

[xlii] *Diagram 10.* Original picture from Thinking in Systems: A primer. Chelsea Green Publishing. 2008.

[xliii] Meadows, Donella. Thinking in Systems: A primer. Chelsea Green Publishing. 2008.

[xliv] *Diagram 11.* Original picture from Thinking in Systems: A primer. Chelsea Green Publishing. 2008.

[xlv] Meadows, Donella. Thinking in Systems: A primer. Chelsea Green Publishing. 2008.

[xlvi] Meadows, Donella. Thinking in Systems: A primer. Chelsea Green Publishing. 2008.

[xlvii] *Diagram 12.* Original picture from Thinking in Systems: A primer. Chelsea Green Publishing. 2008.

[xlviii] Chatteerjee, Pratap. Dick Cheney's Halliburton: a corporate case study. The Guardian. 2011.
https://www.theguardian.com/commentisfree/cifameric
a/2011/jun/08/dick-cheney-halliburton-supreme-court

[xlix] I See Systems. Applying Systems Thinking and Common Archetypes to Organizational Issues. Module 6: Systems Archetypes. 2018.
https://www.iseesystems.com/Online_training/course/
module6/6-02-0-0-what.htm

[l] Meadows, Donella. Thinking in Systems: A primer. Chelsea Green Publishing. 2008.

[li] Hale, David M. Behind the bling: The story of Clemson's epic championship rings. ESPN. 2017.
http://www.espn.com/college-
football/story/_/id/20466841/clemson-tigers-dabo-

swinney-big-business-college-football-championship-rings

[lii] *Diagram 13*. Original Picture from I See Systems. Applying Systems Thinking and Common Archetypes to Organizational Issues. Module 6: Systems Archetypes. Implications & Leverage Points. Success to the Successful. I See Systems. 2018. https://www.iseesystems.com/Online_training/course/module6/6-13-3-0-successimp.htm

[liii] Herbert, Christopher E. Haurin , Donald R. Rosenthal, Stuart S. Duda, Mark. Homeownership Gaps Among Low-Income and Minority Borrowers and Neighborhoods. U.S. Department of Housing and Urban Development. 2005. https://www.huduser.gov/Publications/pdf/HomeownershipGapsAmongLow-IncomeAndMinority.pdf

[liv] Beattie, Andrwe. Why Buying in Bulk Doesn't Always Save You Money. Investopedia. 2018. https://www.investopedia.com/articles/pf/07/bulk_buying.asp

[lv] *Diagram 14*. Original picture from I See Systems. Applying Systems Thinking and Common Archetypes to Organizational Issues. Module 6: Systems Archetypes. Implications & Leverage Points. Success to the Successful. I See Systems. 2018. https://www.iseesystems.com/Online_training/course/module6/6-13-3-0-successimp.htm

[lvi] I See Systems. Applying Systems Thinking and Common Archetypes to Organizational Issues. Module 6: Systems Archetypes. Implications & Leverage Points. Success to the Successful. I See Systems. 2018. https://www.iseesystems.com/Online_training/course/module6/6-13-3-0-successimp.htm

[lvii] *Diagram 15.* I See Systems. Original picture from Applying Systems Thinking and Common Archetypes to Organizational Issues. Module 6: Systems Archetypes. Implications & Leverage Points. Escalation. I See Systems. 2018.
https://www.iseesystems.com/Online_training/course/module6/6-11-3-0-escalimp.htm

[lviii] Meadows, Donella. Thinking in Systems: A primer. Chelsea Green Publishing. 2008.

[lix] *Diagram 16.* Original picture from I See Systems. Applying Systems Thinking and Common Archetypes to Organizational Issues. Module 6: Systems Archetypes. Implications & Leverage Points. Shifting the Burden. I See Systems. 2018.
https://www.iseesystems.com/Online_training/course/module6/6-06-3-0-shiftimp.htm

[lx] I See Systems. Applying Systems Thinking and Common Archetypes to Organizational Issues. Module 6: Systems Archetypes. Implications & Leverage Points. Shifting the Burden. I See Systems. 2018.
https://www.iseesystems.com/Online_training/course/module6/6-06-3-0-shiftimp.htm

[lxi] Stroh, Peter David. Systems Thinking For Social Change. Chelsea Green Publishing. 2015.

[lxii] Onda, Tsuyoshi. Abortion Worldwide 2017: Uneven Progress and Unequal Access. Guttmacher. 2018.
https://www.guttmacher.org/report/abortion-worldwide-2017

[lxiii] Death Penalty Information Center. Deterrence: States Without the Death Penalty Have Had Consistently Lower Murder Rates. Death Penalty Information Center. 2017.
https://deathpenaltyinfo.org/deterrence-states-without-

death-penalty-have-had-consistently-lower-murder-rates
[lxiv] Stroh, Peter David. Systems Thinking For Social Change. Chelsea Green Publishing. 2015.
[lxv] Collaboration for Impact. The Collective Impact Framework. Collaboration for Impact. 2018. https://www.collaborationforimpact.com/collective-impact/
[lxvi] Stroh, Peter David. Systems Thinking For Social Change. Chelsea Green Publishing. 2015.
[lxvii] *Diagram 17*. Original picture from Northwest Earth Institute. A Systems Thinking Model: The Iceberg. Northwest Earth Institute. 2018. https://www.nwei.org/iceberg/
[lxviii] Gerber, John. Systems Thinking Tools: Finding The Root Cause(S) Of Big Problems. Changing The Story. 2012. https://changingthestory.net/2012/07/18/rootcaus/
[lxix] Northwest Earth Institute. A Systems Thinking Model: The Iceberg. Northwest Earth Institute. 2018. https://www.nwei.org/iceberg/
[lxx] Durose, Matthew. Cooper, Alexia D. Ph.D., Snyder, Howard N. Ph.D. Recidivism of Prisoners Released in 30 States in 2005: Patterns from 2005 to 2010. U.S. Department of Justice. 2014. https://www.bjs.gov/content/pub/pdf/rprts05p0510.pdf
[lxxi] Pryser Libell, Henrik. Anders Behring Breivik, Killer in 2011 Norway Massacre, Says Prison Conditions Violate His Rights. The New York Times. 2016. https://www.nytimes.com/2016/03/16/world/europe/anders-breivik-nazi-prison-lawsuit.html
[lxxii] Sterbenz, Christina. Why Norway's prison system is so successful. Business Insider. 2014.

https://www.businessinsider.com/why-norways-prison-system-is-so-successful-2014-12/?IR=T

[lxxiii] World Prison Brief. Highest to Lowest. Prison Population Total. World Prison Brief. 2018.
http://www.prisonstudies.org/highest-to-lowest/prison-population-total?field_region_taxonomy_tid=All

[lxxiv] Martin, Will. The 31 safest countries in the world. Business Insider. 2018.
https://www.businessinsider.my/safest-countries-in-the-world-2018-6/?r=US&IR=T

[lxxv] Stroh, Peter David. Systems Thinking For Social Change. Chelsea Green Publishing. 2015.

[lxxvi] Kubish C, Anne. Structural Racism. Racial Equity Tools. 2006.
www.racialequitytools.org/resourcefiles/kubisch.pdf

[lxxvii] Stroh, Peter David. Goodman, Michael. A Systemic Approach to Ending Homelessness. Applied Systems Thinking. 2007.
http://www.appliedsystemsthinking.com/supporting_documents/TopicalHomelessness.pdf

[lxxviii] Stroh, Peter David. Goodman, Michael. A Systemic Approach to Ending Homelessness. Applied Systems Thinking. 2007.
http://www.appliedsystemsthinking.com/supporting_documents/TopicalHomelessness.pdf

[lxxix] *Diagram 19*. Original picture from Stroh, Peter David. Goodman, Michael. A Systemic Approach to Ending Homelessness. Applied Systems Thinking. 2007.
http://www.appliedsystemsthinking.com/supporting_documents/TopicalHomelessness.pdf

[lxxx] Stroh, Peter David. Goodman, Michael. A Systemic Approach to Ending Homelessness. Applied Systems Thinking. 2007.

http://www.appliedsystemsthinking.com/supporting_d
ocuments/TopicalHomelessness.pdf

[lxxxi] Zurcher, Kathleen. Stroh, Peter David. Acting and
Thinking Systemically. The Systems Thinker. 2018.
https://thesystemsthinker.com/acting-and-thinking-
systemically/

[lxxxii] Battle Creek Michigan. Homeless Coalition
discusses local facts on health fair day. Battle Creek
Michigan. 2017.
https://www.battlecreekmi.gov/CivicAlerts.aspx?AID=
505&ARC=624

[lxxxiii] Stroh, Peter David. Systems Thinking For Social
Change. Chelsea Green Publishing. 2015.

[lxxxiv] Kushinka, Matthew. Countries That Start with D:
There's Something Rotten in America. Red Lines.
2018. https://www.redlinels.com/countries-start-d/

[lxxxv] Collen, Arne. Minati, Gianfranco. Seven Activities
To Engage Systems Thinking. Semantic Scholar. 1997.
https://pdfs.semanticscholar.org/3436/c52688ab6dae54
5fdb783bb0b88b8b052c16.pdf

[lxxxvi] Collen, Arne. Minati, Gianfranco. Seven
Activities To Engage Systems Thinking. Semantic
Scholar. 1997.
https://pdfs.semanticscholar.org/3436/c52688ab6dae54
5fdb783bb0b88b8b052c16.pdf

[lxxxvii] Booth Sweeney, Linda. Meadows, Dennis. The
Systems Thinking Playbook. Chelsea Green
Publishing. 2010.

[lxxxviii] Booth Sweeney, Linda. Meadows, Dennis. The
Systems Thinking Playbook. Chelsea Green
Publishing. 2010.

[lxxxix] Meadows, Donella. Thinking in Systems: A
primer. Chelsea Green Publishing. 2008.

[xc] Stroh, Peter David. Systems Thinking For Social Change. Chelsea Green Publishing. 2015.